With the Royal Engineers in the Low Countries

With the Royal Engineers in the Low Countries

At Bergen-op-Zoom, Waterloo and the Advance

on Paris, 1813-15

ILLUSTRATED

Letters of an Officer of the Royal Engineers

to His Father

John Sperling

With Two Short Accounts of the Royal Engineers
and Royal Sappers and Miners During this Period

by Whitworth Porter & T. W. J. Connolly

LEONAUR

With the Royal Engineers in the Low Countries
At Bergen-op-Zoom, Waterloo and the Advance on Paris, 1813-15
Letters of an Officer of the Royal Engineers to His Father
John Sperling
With Two Short Accounts of the Royal Engineers and Royal Sappers and Miners
During this Period
by Whitworth Porter & T. W. J. Connolly

ILLUSTRATED

FIRST EDITION IN THIS FORM

First published under the titles
Letters of an Officer of the Royal Engineers to His Father
and
Extracts from *History of the Royal Engineers* and H*istory of the Sappers and Miners*

Leonaur is an imprint of Oakpast Ltd
Copyright in this form © 2023 Oakpast Ltd

ISBN: 978-1-916535-72-5 (hardcover)
ISBN: 978-1-916535-73-2 (softcover)

http://www.leonaur.com

Publisher's Notes

Contents

To the Reader

The existence of the following letters requires some explanation.

On looking over the papers of my father, at his decease, I found all my letters preserved.

Some time since it occurred to me to examine them, with a view to their destruction. I became, however, interested in the journal, and set about transcribing it, which was accomplished in the leisure afforded by autumnal visits to relatives.

Friends to whom I showed the manuscripts expressed gratification in the perusal. Talking with a valued acquaintance, familiar with literary pursuits, of what I had been doing, he desired to see the letters, and returned them with warm suggestions for their publication.

From similar observations, the result is that the letters are now committed to the press with some diffidence, but not without a humble trust that it may please God to accompany them with His blessing.

John Sperling.

Kensington Palace Gardens.

Introduction

Chatham had been my station for a short time, when, in November, 1813, several of the officers of Engineers received orders to hold themselves in readiness for immediate foreign service. Included in this number were Hayter and myself. Having been on the Ordnance Survey together, and afterwards obtained our commissions in December, 1811, we had lived very much in each other's society. This was mutually advantageous, and our intimacy tended both to our profit and enjoyment. Dining at the mess, our other meals were in common, taking them alternately at each other's rooms.

In forwarding our orders from Pall Mall, Colonel Handfield had kindly enclosed a private note, directing us to come to London, to provide the necessary equipments.

Holland, we learnt was to be our destination. The Dutch had availed themselves of the disastrous termination of Buonaparte's Russian expedition, which necessitated the recruiting of his army from the various garrisons quartered in their different towns, to assert their national independence, and turn against their oppressors.

The drafts for the French Army had only been partially replaced by recruits. Upon the rising of the Dutch, the French who remained were obliged to concentrate themselves in the principal fortifications.

The Dutch had applied to England for the aid of a force to protect them and confirm their independence.

The visit to London gave us an opportunity of taking leave of our friends who were not far off. My grandmother gave me all the guineas she possessed, which proved very useful afterwards. In those days of one-pound notes, gold was not to be had. We posted back to Chatham the following day, with our various purchases, there to await our final order.

This soon followed, directing us to proceed to Ramsgate for embarkation. Arriving at Ramsgate we took up our quarters at an hotel.

The wind being unfavourable, the transports not collected, we engaged a lodging. A mess was also arranged at an inn where we assembled for dinner.

The Engineer officers appointed for the expedition were Lieut.-Colonel Carmichael Smyth, commanding; Captain Sir George Hoste, Captain Thompson, commanding the Sappers and Miners; Lieutenants Abbey, appointed Adjutant and Quartermaster, Sperling, Hayter, White, Cooper, Eyre; Sub-Lieutenant Adamson, of the Sappers and Miners. He, with the company, was stationed at Margate.

The delay at Ramsgate was very needful for organising the different departments of the service, and the various portions of regiments collected from the several depots.

Sir Thomas Graham, afterwards Lord Lynedoch, was Commander-in-Chief; under him Major-Generals Cooke, Mackenzie, and Skerret.

It was our happiness to find Colonel Foy, of the Royal Horse Artillery, with Mrs. Foy, at Ramsgate, whose kindness made our stay very pleasant.

It may impart an interest to these letters to say a word of the late Major-General Sir James Carmichael Smyth, Bart., C.B., K.C.H., K.M.T., and K.S.W., whose name so frequently occurs, from the position the writer occupied under him. It was not, indeed, then clothed with the honours with which, afterwards, his services were so deservedly recognised, but as simply Lieut.-Colonel.

It is a satisfaction to pay a grateful tribute to the memory of one whose uniform kindness was experienced by the writer during their military connection. When that ceased with the breaking up of the Army of Occupation in France, in 1818, it was followed by a pleasant intercourse, kept up either personally or by writing.

I have now before me an interesting letter detailing his very useful labours in the Government of British Guiana, where, after having effected a great reformation, he was suddenly cut off by fever in the year 1838.

After the army was withdrawn from France, the Duke of Wellington entrusted to him to report upon our West Indian possessions and defences; afterwards on Canada, which met with so much approbation that his statement was ordered to be printed for Government circulation.

In the recently published volume of the Supplementary Despatches of the Duke of Wellington, there is a Minute dated 1st May, 1827, relative to extra pay, which indicates that great man's estimate of Sir

James Carmichael Smyth. His Grace says —

"These matters must always be considered in reference to the precedent likely to be created, particularly when they relate to a man of such high character as Sir J. C. Smyth.

"His services and opinions have been so useful since his return from his commissions in the West Indies and in Canada, as to be absolutely necessary."

A FIELD OFFICER of ROYAL ENGINEERS,
and A PRIVATE SAPPER.

Letters of an Officer of the Corps of Royal Engineers

1

Northash Schooner, at anchor, Downs,
Dec. 11th, 1813.

My dear Father,

I made a hurried attempt early this morning to write a few lines, hearing that a boat was going into the harbour; it was off, however, before the letter was ready. I now sit down to write more leisurely, to avail myself of the next opportunity.

It may be necessary to preface that my head is all in a whirl from the constant shaking of our little schooner, which brings forcibly to mind the blessings of the shore. How little we appreciate our blessings till we feel what it is to be deprived of them. I purpose keeping a sort of journal, with the hope that it may remind me of the mercies of God; by His Grace may my heart feel gratitude to the great Giver of all good. I have derived some consolation this morning from the perusal of Jonah's prayer in the fish's belly, and never was so sensible to the beauty of the Prophet's description of his wretched situation.

I commence the journal from the—

9th Dec, 1813.—We had now been delayed about a fortnight at Ramsgate. Hayter and myself were engaged to dine at Colonel Foy's to meet Captain Nicholls and a clergyman from Canterbury. As, however, we were setting down to breakfast at our lodgings, Captain Thompson's servant brought a message that his master wished to see me immediately. From him I learnt that there were orders for our embarkation at 11 o'clock. He directed me to go to Margate to bring over the company of Sappers, and get the men ready for embarkation. Hiring a horse, I rode to Margate.

As all was ready for marching, the captain himself appeared and took charge of the men, while he set me at liberty to return to get my luggage ready; which having done, the company arrived. We were hurried on board without any opportunity of making a food provision; the day being rainy added to the bustle. Everything was, however, ready, and we sailed out of the harbour that tide.

The vessel in which we are stowed is the *Northash*, a small schooner, built for and employed in the coal trade, therefore quite unsuitable for the purpose for which it is now used. One small cabin, usually occupied by the master, containing two berths and hooks for swinging a cot over the centre, is allotted to us. The men are worse off, as they have only the hold, where the coals are stowed, and which still retains their dust. There seems no provision for their sleeping but their one blanket. We soon reached the Downs, where we came to anchor.

Captain Thompson and myself are the only officers of Engineers on board. Sub-Lieutenant Adamson of the Sappers makes the third in our cabin. As night drew on, it blew a gale. I became very sick. Captain T. and his servant were more accustomed to the sea, but my lad Davis was worse than myself. Adamson is an old soldier, and the sea had no effect upon him. He made himself of great use to us, and kindly prepared my berth, making it as comfortable as two blankets and my large cloak would allow. Captain T. swung his cot. Adamson moving the table out of the cabin, the two lads spread their blankets on the floor, under the captain's cot, while he himself occupied the other berth. What with the hardness of the bed, the rolling and creaking of the vessel, and my own state, sleep could not be expected.

Friday, 10th Dec.—The wind continued very fresh. Many of the transports returned to Ramsgate. Our master had some thoughts of doing the same; but in this we were disappointed, it being decided to ride the gale out.

11th Dec,—Better night, more comfortable in myself, and falling into my new mode of life. Captain Thompson has a large and well-stocked canteen, in which he kindly makes us share. From the suddenness of the embarkation, and ignorance of what the ship supplied as rations, I had laid in no stock. We are now boiling some of the ship beef, to try what we can make of it.

Your kind letter reached me as I was embarking. I am thankful that I have the prayers of you all, that I may walk worthy of our Father in Heaven, and be kept by His power from evil.

12th, Sunday Morning,—An opportunity offers of sending my letter. There seems a prospect of sailing, as we are to work up against the wind.

With love, &c., I am, &c.,   J. S.

2

Northash Transport, off Helvoetsluys,
Dec. 15th, 1813.

My dear Father,

After a pleasanter voyage than anticipated, we came to anchor early this morning, and are waiting the arrival of the other transports. In the tackings of the river we find the advantage of our smaller vessel, as we now take the lead, whereas in the open sea we were always in the rear of the decked ships.

Hayter and the other officers were to have embarked the day after us, but the stormy weather not permitting, they left the harbour on Saturday, and came to anchor a little distance from us. I had the pleasure of seeing him in a boat alongside of our vessel. The weather had become more favourable, and everything wore a more pleasant aspect, even our salt beef, for we depend on the rations. Captain T. went ashore. The Dutch express great joy at our arrival. Provisions are much cheaper than in England: butter, 8*d.* per lb.; beef, 5½*d.*; but tea and sugar are exorbitant; for coffee, substitutes only are to be had.

I inquired of the Dutch pilot, who has taken the charge of our vessel up the river, if he knew the Cremers. He said, very well, and that they still reside at Rotterdam. In consequence of intelligence of the evacuation of the country by the French, Sir Thomas Graham has, we hear, with his staff, taken the course of the Scheldt.

16th.—We sailed for Wilhemstadt, which we reached in the afternoon, the other transports not arriving till the following morning.

Captain T. took me with him into the town to report our arrival to Major-General Cooke, who is in command, he having entered by the Scheldt. We were introduced by the Dutch officer commanding the Artillery, and received with much civility.

Never having seen a Dutch town, its novelty was striking: the neat and cleanly appearance, the brick-paved paths, rows of trees, gabled houses, also the manners, dress, and high coloured faces of the inhabitants, all so different from England. We entered several shops, but, ignorant of the language, our intercourse was very limited.

The town is small, but strongly fortified, and important as a mili-

15

SIR THOMAS GRAHAM

tary position. That the French should have given up its arsenal and stores, shows the importance they felt in concentrating their scattered forces. The report of our approach had precipitated the evacuation, and not allowed them to effect the destruction they proposed, the preparations for which were manifest. Some of the ships were scuttled, but the arsenal and its effects seemed little injured.

17th Dec.—The infantry was disembarking all day, and as the town could not contain them, the greater part marched for Tholen. None but those disembarking were allowed to quit their ships today.

18th Dec, Saturday,—About noon we were ordered on shore; the horses were landed at the same time. I have omitted to mention that Colonel Foy, in addition to his other attentions, purchased a horse for me at Canterbury, which reached Ramsgate as they were embarking.

As we landed, we received orders to leave the town for Headquarters; all the accommodation was wanted for those whose duties detained them, and for those disembarking later in the day. We therefore broke up our saddlery boxes on the landing place, and accoutred our horses; those who had no horses were to follow with the Sappers and baggage.

Our party consisted of Captain Thompson, Abbey, Cooper, and self. Tholen, where Sir Thomas Graham and Colonel Smyth were, was our destination. The resting place for the night was Steinbergen, about 10 miles distant. Rain had set in: the road which lay along the dyke was in a wretched state, from the previous traffic; the horses frequently could scarcely walk from the depth of mud. We had some difficulty in tracking the way, from our ignorance of the country, and the peculiar arrangement of the roads following the dykes. Night overtaking us, added to our perplexities.

We were delighted at length to find ourselves in a town. Here, however, new troubles awaited us in obtaining accommodation, the place being already occupied by those preceding us.

The *burgomaster*, however, referring to his lists, gave us billets (or orders for lodging) for ourselves upon different houses. As the stables were all occupied, a large empty building or magazine was allotted for the horses. Orders were given us on stores, situated in different parts of the town, for hay, corn, and straw, which we had to fetch upon our own shoulders. This occupied some time, from the darkness and our ignorance of the language and the ways. We had previously tied up our horses to some pillars in the magazine, and now having cleaned

SIR JAMES CARMICHAEL SMYTH

down and fed our muddy beasts, we went in search of our respective habitations for the night.

My billet proved a very comfortable one; instead of being looked upon as an unwelcome intruder at that late hour, I was received with a kind welcome. It was a shop for threads, tapes, and such like, kept by two females, who from the popularity of the English, as their liberators from oppression, had shown me so much good will. They left nothing undone which could contribute to my comfort. As they spoke French we were enabled to converse together.

19th December, Sunday,—Breakfasted with my kind entertainers, who were Roman Catholics, but so mingled with Protestants that there were only a few symbols to show it. They declined to receive any payment at my departure, though pressed.

Being obliged to resume our route, we prepared our horses and set off for Tholen. We passed near Bergen-op-Zoom, still occupied by the French, reaching our destination about noon.

Our first object was to be lodged, so we went to the *burgomaster* for billets for ourselves and horses, which were supplied to us. Several successive ones which I received were occupied, for the town was pretty well filled with men and horses. The horse was, however, accommodated. Returning to the *burgomaster* he directed me to go to one of the houses on which I had received a billet, where two officers had been billeted, but one had left, and tell the master of the house he must receive me for the present. Later in the day I should have another billet, when some should have left the town.

The master of the house, a respectable old gentleman, was at dinner with his family, of which, with much civility, he asked me to partake, though naturally he could not help manifesting his distress that a second officer should have been allotted to his house. When the cloth was removed, he had recourse to his pipe, and I having forage to provide for the horse, thanking him, took leave.

I fell in with Colonel Smyth, who had been admitted blindfold into Bergen-op-Zoom with a flag of truce to induce the *commandant* to surrender, who declined, stating he was fully prepared for an attack. He was with Sir Thos. Graham. I made also an acquaintance with Lieutenant Pringle of the Artillery.

Disappointed in another attempt at obtaining a billet, there was no alternative but to return to the old gentleman's house, however uncomfortable to my own feelings, who I found still over the fire smoking his pipe, with tea before him. He was evidently discomposed and vexed at my reappearance, apprehensive that he would have to lodge me for the night.

The house within and without and his style of living showed that he was in easy circumstances. Though so impatient of my stay, he invited me to join the tea-table. At length night drawing on, to relieve his increasing restlessness I rose up to make another appeal to the *burgomaster*, and he resumed his pipe, which in his discomposure he had laid aside.

My interview with the *burgomaster* was successful, and I received a billet, which proves a very comfortable one, placing me again amongst kind and accommodating people, quite a contrast to the old gentleman I had left, but inferior in their position of life. The mistress of the house is an elderly person, a widow of very respectable appearance. As she speaks only Dutch, we have no medium of communication; but as far as we can understand each other she is one of those termed by the apostle widows indeed.

The apartment allotted to me is an old-fashioned room, its walls covered with stamped and gilded leather, which, though it has lost its brilliancy, has a very comfortable appearance. A recess near the fireplace, closed with folding doors, contains the bed. The room is adorned with little china figures. It had been vacated the preceding part of the day by Sir George Hoste, who had been detached elsewhere. I need hardly remark this was Sunday, of which, indeed, there was no indication from the general bustle in the streets and the open shops.

20th December.—About noon the company of sappers, with the other officers,, servants, and baggage, arrived. Hayter finding the same difficulty I had experienced in getting billeted, my kind hostess willingly received him into her house.

21st December,—Colonel Smyth sent Capt. Thompson with Hayter to superintend the disembarkation of the ordnance stores at Williamstadt. I have charge of the company, with the exception of those employed at Williamstadt. Rode to look round Bergen-op-Zoom. My horse was dislodged for the accommodation of Major-General Cooke, and not without difficulty another place was found.

Rations are now issued to the officers and men daily, or as now being stationary for three days at a time. The daily ration consists of a pound of beef, one and a-half pound of brown bread, a small quan-

SIR GEORGE CHARLES HOSTE

tity of spirits, a portion of fuel according to rank, and forage for our horses. My hostess, who is full of kind offices, receives the rations and prepares our food. The servants have the same rations as the soldiers. Tholen is a larger town than Williamstadt, with some good houses in it, and surrounded with earthen fortifications. The picquets and light troops are encompassing Bergen-op-Zoom. It is only about three miles from hence.

I wrote from the Downs, and entrusted the letter to a boatman who came alongside with provisions. I am encompassed by a multitude of mercies. A bag of letters for England is making up, so conclude with many kind loves.

Yours, &c.,   J. S.

Tholen, 22nd December, 1813.

3

Standaardhuyten,
January 3, 1814.

My dear Father,

I continue a sort of journal from the time the last letter was sent from Tholen under a cover to Colonel Handfield. I am not able to supply you with any intelligence beyond that which passes under my own notice. Every movement and its object is withheld from all but those immediately concerned. You hear, probably, better in England what is going on than we do in Holland.

24th December, 1813.—Orders were issued from headquarters to move to Steenbergen, and the following day to Williamstadt. This unexpected retrograde movement we understood was in consequence of the advance of a French force which was thought to have in view some of those places which had been so suddenly evacuated, which made the protection of Williamstadt important where the stores are landing. A small garrison is left in Tholen. However, it appears that the object of the French was to reinforce the garrison of Bergen-op-Zoom and to supply provisions. Having charge of the Sappers, I accompanied them to Steenbergen, where we halted for the night. Moving with H. Q. there are so many horses to be accommodated that it is difficult to get stable room, and it was now a troublesome affair.

Abbey and myself were billeted on the same house, and we slept in the same room. The house seemed a species of hotel. They were very civil, and provided comfortably for us. When, however, we came to settle we found their charges excessive; a payment also for our lodging was asked for, which of course was refused.

25th, Christmas-day,—Marched in the morning for Williamstadt. The road was as before, or worse, but we had the advantage of daylight, and it did not rain. The greater number of the men pulled off shoes, gaiters, and stockings to get through the mud. The wheels of the artillery and waggons were continually one sheet of mud, so that the spokes were not visible.

On our arrival, about four o'clock, the men were crowded into barracks. The little town being already overfilled, the prospect was not very favourable for our night accommodation. Finding Colonel Smyth, he interested himself for us, and Abbey and I got into a house occupied by other officers, but there was an uninhabited back room on the ground vacant, in which, notwithstanding its dampness, we were glad to make up our beds. The owner of the house also made room for our horses, and the servants found a sleeping-place upon some hay in the stable.

26th Dec, Sunday.—Employed great part of the day in superintending the formation of a landing-place for the artillery!!

27th Dec.—Marched in the morning to the village of Klundert, happy to bid farewell to our uncomfortable abode. Received a billet upon a poor man's house, which finding already occupied by some soldiers round the one fire, I was obliged to get a billet for them elsewhere. Being thus quit of the soldiers, was a great boon to my poor hosts. They were able to spare me a small sleeping-room, opening into the general room by the ascent of a few steps. The general cleanliness of the Dutch is a great comfort, for whatever may be the annoyances, filth is not one of them.

There was no reason to regret the poor accommodation of my host's house, for he was rich in better things, and seemed filled with a spirit of deep and ardent piety, which diffused itself throughout his whole family.

29th Dec.—How lovely a sight to witness a household in their circumstances so influenced by religion. Serious devotion was conspicuous in the man, not only when engaged in religious services, but throughout all his occupations, and from them and his work (a shoemaker) he seemed to return with fresh zest to his Bible.

****

I know not how to pass over this page without taking note of the po-

ARTILLERY DRIVERS SHOWING WAGGONS OF THE PERIOD

sition of the poor shoemaker. His time must have been of great value to him, yet he has no hesitation in giving it up to God, for he looked "at the things which are not seen," and "which are eternal."

What a sad contrast, may we not say awful, did the state of our army present in those days, an ignoring of all the external obligations of Christianity. We had been ten days in the country. Two Sundays and Christmas-day had passed without the smallest recognition. Must not this public casting-off of God seriously affect the moral conduct of the soldier?

★★★★★★★★★★

A devout grace preceded every meal, and a chapter of the Bible the morning and evening family prayers. We found an occasional interpreter in a neighbour, a native of Scotland. In the room were many religious books, chiefly translations from standard English works.

In the evening I received orders to take a detachment of sappers to construct a bridge of boats at Standaardhuyten.

30th Dec.—Left Klundert before dawn with 45 men. My kind hosts seemed to regret my departure, but such is military life, friendly interests are formed but for the moment.

It was a fine frosty morning, which made it pleasant to march with the men, so put the servant with some luggage on the horse. We reached our destination early.

Standaardhuyten is a straggling village situated at the ferry over the River Dintel, by which it is separated from Oudenbosch, a small town a mile and a half distant. The village was already occupied. Having got the men accommodated, I could only get a billet for myself at a distant farmhouse, which was too far from my work. The ferryman, who had a house on an island on the Oudenbosch side of the river, offered to take me in. It being so convenient for my work, the offer was accepted.

The boats for the bridge were to be sent from different towns up the river; two arrived in the afternoon.

The day closing, I entered my new quarters at the ferry-house. There was a spacious room upstairs, which was the living room of the family, a reception-room for all visitors, and had the appearance of being occasionally used by pleasure parties. It also served for the accommodation of those who might be detained by any obstruction in passing the river. The ferryman was a stout, jolly fellow, but not the most civilized; his wife appeared more shrewd.

A round table was spread in the middle of the room for the family supper. I was invited to a chair. Two other men made up our party. The fare consisted of a tureen of milk soup and a dish of potatoes with melted butter. Our host then drew from his pocket a large clasp knife, with which he cut a portion of bread for each. All then proceeded to dip their spoons in the milk till the bowl was quickly emptied in this primitive way. I was reminded of the text, "He that dippeth his hand with me in the dish." The ferryman was quite a contrast to the shoemaker.

The sleeping-rooms were on the ground floor; the one allotted to myself and servant was an ante-room to that of our hosts. A sudden thaw had made the room wet and everything in it very damp. There was only one blanket, which I gave to the lad, and he slept upon some chairs. I was afraid of doing anything more than wrapping myself in the cloak, which is happily interlined with oilskin, which prevented the wet penetrating, but the blanket might have been wrung out.

31st Dec,—By the exertions of Abbey, our adjutant, the previous day, enough boats had arrived during the night for stretching across the river. By break of day, we were at work, only ceasing with the night. There were five boats and the wherry, which obliged us to place them further apart than should have been done could more have been obtained. The other materials were chiefly procured from Oudenbosch. Considering the preparation of the materials, credit was due to the men for the zeal with which they worked. In the course of the afternoon, it was fit for the passage of cavalry. Sir Thomas Graham passed over first, accompanied by the colonel, who gave me an expression of satisfaction. Afterwards cavalry and waggons followed.

1st Jan. 1814,—Employed making additions to the bridge for its strength and security, and preparing materials for a smaller one over a stream flowing from Oudenbosch into the Dintel.

2nd Jan,—Sunday passes undistinguished from other days, its sanctity disregarded and lost sight of in the usual routine of work. One feels it the more where there is no place for retirement. The inhabitants of the wherry-house are Roman Catholics, of whom there are many in this neighbourhood.

3rd Jan,—Completed the smaller bridge over the stream from Oudenbosch, the centre part of which was made moveable to admit the passage of vessels. It was supported by piles, and was 72 feet in length.

I began to be very tired of my hosts and their accommodation. The frost leaving, the bedroom resumed its dampness. The large room was continually occupied by men dropping in for refreshment. In the evening it was the station of the officer commanding the picquet guard. The woman who provided my food was also very overreaching, and obliged me to have recourse to the *burgomaster* of Oudenbosch for redress. As my proximity to the bridge had not now the same importance, I took up my billet at the farmhouse, which, though a mile distant, is very preferable in every other respect. I have a very comfortable room.

From the thaw which had taken place the ice came down the river in large sheets with much force. Being apprehensive that the cables would be cut, piles were driven in at the heads of the boats to serve as a fender.

Some of the men were employed in restoring an ancient *tête du pont* which had formerly served as a protection for the passage of the river. Colonel Smyth came this afternoon, and expressed his satisfaction with what had been done.

4th Jan.—The men were employed at the *tête du pont* with the addition of some country labourers. Taken unwell in the afternoon, probably arising from the former accommodation, standing about in the wet, and exposed to the sleet.

5th and 6th Jan.—Did not leave the house; its inhabitants were very obliging, quite a contrast to those of the ferry-house. My room was very comfortable.

7th Jan.—Being, thank God, re-established, visited the bridge. The frost had returned. There had been a very high tide. The river had overflowed its banks. One of the boats had sunk; this was replaced by another and the damage repaired. I rode over to Colonel Smyth at Klundert, returning by Zevenbergen to get another boat in case of further damage. Zevenbergen is a very pretty little town. In summer the dykes with the avenues of trees along the river must have a pretty effect.

8th and 9th Jan.—Collecting the bills on account of the bridge. Having learnt at Headquarters that waggons would no longer be allowed for officers' baggage, I bought a horse and light cart.

Orders in the evening to march the men to Rosendaal in the morning. Headquarters would also move thither from Klundert.

10th Jan.—We left Standaardhuyten at dawn, very cold, arriving at Rosendaal by eleven. Being already occupied, much was not to be expected in the way of accommodation. Rosendaal is a large, open, pleasant village, with many good houses.

11th Jan.—I resume the pen, my dearest father, soon after midnight, to say that about half an hour ago a messenger from the colonel aroused me from my bed with an order to come to him. He gave me instructions to take the command of twenty sappers and march in rear of a column that leaves this at 2 o'clock a.m.

I understand a skirmish is expected with the French, who have a force at a little distance.

May God, our gracious Lord, give me in all things a firm dependence upon Him, who is, I trust, my sure sanctuary and refuge. May He bless you and my dear mother with every blessing. Should it please Him that I should not return to you, I hope you will take care that my servant is put to some good trade.

With love, &c.,   J. S,

4

Headquarters, Oudenbosch,
17th Jan., 1814.

My dear Father,

Understanding that a bag of letters for England is to be sealed this evening, I hasten not to lose the opportunity. I concluded my last when leaving Rosendaal, but no bag seems to have been made up, so that it will be received with this.

11th Jan.—At the appointed hour, 2 o'clock a.m., we were in marching order. As no baggage was to be taken, Davis, whom I now find very useful, was left behind. The artillery had their matches lighted. We understood the object of this movement was to take in flank and rear a French force which had been advancing on Breda, and thus intercept their retreat on Antwerp, while the Prussians assailed them in front.

Passing through Nispen and Aspen we, reached Calmthout. Here we came to a halt. Some of the light troops went forward, but nothing was seen of the enemy, though the firing was distinctly heard. The severe frost had made the roads very pleasant, but it was bitterly cold standing about the whole day. Returned with my detachment to Nispen in the evening.

I fell in with Sir George Hoste, the Engineer officer attached to Major-General Cooke's division, halting here for the night, who kindly made me a sharer in his billet, a good sized room, made very comfortable by a large wood fire. During the night, while we slept, the sentinel at our door was charged to have it kept up.

12th Jan.—Left Nispen at four in the morning, after a comfortable basin of coffee and milk. We advanced in rear of Major-General Cooke's division a few miles beyond Calmthout. Halting about during the day in suspense, we returned to the village of Calmthout for the night, occupying the same billet with Sir George Hoste. The troops were lodged in the villages around.

13th Jan.—Marched again at four a.m. The cold intense. Fall of snow. Halted at Capelle. The infantry advanced upon Antwerp, falling in with the French at the village of Merxem, close upon Antwerp, where they had halted and strengthened their position by throwing trees across the road and making loopholes in the walls and houses. After some sharp skirmishing they retired under the fortifications of Antwerp. As nothing further could be done, our men returned. The object of the French sortie had been frustrated. We lost three or four officers and some men. Many deserters came in during the evening. At Capelle for the night in the same billet with Sir G. Hoste.

14th Jan.—The army returned to its cantonments and I to my former billet at Rosendaal, with my twenty sappers.

17th Jan.—The two intervening days were employed superintending the deposit of the various Engineer stores, which the waggons had brought from Williamstadt. Having received orders to resume the work at the *tête du pont* at Standaardhuyten, took the men over to Oudenbosch, whither Headquarters had moved yesterday.

&c.,   J. S.

5

Breda, Jan. 24th, 1814.

My Dearest Father,

On the 19th I received two letters from you, the first since I have been in Holland, and one from Clifton, for which I thank you. One thing only seems to require an answer in your letters, which has reference to Lady Curtis. As to the invitation to dinner on Sunday, you know that it is correct, but I never received any other invitation from Her Ladyship. I remember that something was said upon balls in conversation which might have been intended as an invitation, but I thought her ladyship seemed in some measure to agree with me, though I never gave as a reason for not going to them that I did not dance.

I am thankful in having an interest in all your prayers. "As thy day is, so shall thy strength be." Well, is it when the promises of Scripture have an influence and are felt in their preciousness, with a conscience sprinkled with the blood of Jesus.

18th Jan,—To resume journal. Went over this morning to the bridge, which is about a mile distant, where the men were variously employed in restoring the former *tête du pont* assisted by some peasants in renewing the ditch and parapet. The making of the fascines was unpleasant work, as there was more ice than wood upon the twigs.

20th Jan,—Sent to Rosendaal to arrange about the conveyance of Engineer stores to Breda. Called upon Pringle of the Artillery. On my return received orders to proceed early in the morning to Breda, to arrange a place to receive the stores and to take charge of them. Lieutenant White took charge of the bridge.

21st Jan,—Rode to Breda in company with Lieutenant Cole, R.A., who was going thither. Road extremely slippery; obliged to lead our horses part of the way. On arriving called upon the Prussian General Bülow, who occupied the town with his division of the army. He appointed a suitable building in the arsenal well adapted for 'the stores and waggons.

The authorities at the *Stadthouse*, as also the inhabitants, were very obliging. My billet is at a tailor's, where there are two Prussian soldiers. Dined at the principal inn with Captain Gardiner and the other officers of Artillery, who are at Breda on a similar errand with myself in behalf of the Artillery stores.

22nd Jan.—Breda is a more important town than any I have yet seen. There are many good houses, and it is well supplied with shops. Inhabitants 11,000, divided into Protestants and Roman Catholics. It is strongly fortified.

On Sunday I attended the Protestant service at the great church. All the women had each their charcoal footstool. The men kept their hats on, except at some particular times. A bag was taken round during the service and presented to each individual to receive the alms of the congregation.

24th Jan.—My employment is to receive the stores as they arrive and to have them so arranged that the waggons may be ready to move whenever required; they have been arriving each day.' Colonel Smyth rode over from Oudenbosch to see that all was right, leaving directions to be ready for an immediate advance. The stores consist of a quantity of timber adapted for the laying of platforms for artillery, making magazines, and whatever may be required for the construction of field batteries, a quantity of sand-bags, entrenching tools, find so forth. These are all packed in the country waggons, most unfit for their present object, and especially for the Artillery stores.

Not half the number of such waggons as ours would be required. The waggons and horses are levied upon the farmers, who receive a very adequate remuneration. To find accommodation this cold weather for so many horses the drivers are scattered about the different villages, which renders it very troublesome to collect them with any punctuality.

Breda has been chosen as the depot for what is required for the bombardment of the dockyard and arsenal of Antwerp, from the convenience of its situation, the abundant store room it affords, and a good paved road uniting the two towns. I have now about one hundred Engineer waggons, each with two horses.

In a former letter something was said at its conclusion about my lad, who makes himself very handy and useful. Should I, in the good providence of God, not return with him, I wish you to have him put to some trade he may like and to defray any expenses needful for his comfort. I am apprehensive about a scald he had a week ago, which was thought trifling and neglected. We are very badly off for surgeons, or, I ought to say, for their medicines, which remain useless at Williamstadt.

The Prussian soldiers conduct themselves with great rudeness to the inmates of the house.

A stranger and a pilgrim upon the earth, having no certain dwelling-place, that in heart I may be a stranger, knowing that this is not my rest because it is polluted.

J. S., 24th January.

6

Groot Zundert,
31st January, 1814.

My dear Father,
On the evening of the 29th there were orders for advancing early in the morning with the waggons. Up early in the arsenal on the 30th,

expecting we should be on the move soon after six. The weather had suddenly changed from frost to rain and sleet. From the difficulty of collecting the drivers and their dilatoriness it was between one and two before the last waggon had left the arsenal. We follow in the rear of the Prussians, from whom we receive orders. So lengthened was the string of waggons that it reached nearly to Rysbergen, our first day's short stage, which I reached soon after three o'clock, to remain for the night.

Today we have moved to this place, about another three miles. Fifty-eight more waggons with Engineer stores have joined us here, with the remainder of the Sappers: the latter leave us in the morning to go forward.

1st February.—Westwesel. Experienced the same dilatoriness in the drivers, who complain they can get no forage. For the night our waggons are parked in an open space by the roadside. Lieut.-Colonel Gold, who commanded the Artillery with us, went forward to join Sir Thos. Graham, who had advanced to Antwerp by the road we had formerly taken to Merxem, with the light artillery and mortars.

In the way to Westwesel we met several poor families, with what they held most precious, seeking to avoid the miseries attendant upon war. Cows drew their carts, in which were stowed their little children and goods, whilst themselves, with laden backs, walked by the side.

The village itself presented a melancholy sight, testifying to the evils and desolation of an army's march. Half the houses were deserted by their inhabitants, doors open or removed, windows broken, rooms containing nothing but the straw which had served for the beds of the Prussian soldiers, with the remains of large fires upon the hearths made from broken doors, or whatever came to hand.

The houses which had been deserted or left unprotected had been plundered, but those in which the owners remained had fared better. The pretty village church had been made the depository of a great quantity of furniture. I had seen something of the overbearing grossness of the Prussian soldiers to the townspeople in Breda, treating them in their billets as servants. It is sad to see the desolation they leave behind them where they have halted for the night, which makes their approach so dreaded. With us everything is paid for, which gives us a welcome.

My billet is at a farmhouse a little distance from the village; it does not appear to have suffered, having been the billet of some superior officer, which has been its protection. So few officers being with the stores we fare the better. My hosts are very obliging. It must be a comfort to them to find their property respected.

2nd February.—We are waiting here anxiously the result of the engagement of our troops with the French at Merxem, which they have strengthened since our former attack. Our waggons are all ready to move as soon as the information reaches us of the retreat of the French to Antwerp.

7th February.

I am thankful to resume my letter from the same village whence I had so far written, not, however, in the same house, but from the post-house, where six of us are billeted; we occupy the large room of general resort, and are better off than we have been the last few days. To return to my journal.

2nd February.—The French having retired about noon orders reached us to advance to Merxem with the Artillery and Engineer stores. Being prepared, and only waiting instructions, the waggons were put in motion, and we arrived at Merxem about seven in the evening. The stores were deposited about the church. Having reported myself to Colonel Smyth, he gave me directions for the construction of a mortar battery, and to take the Sappers under my charge with me. I understood that Sir G. Hoste, Capt. Thompson, and Cooper had somewhat similar employments elsewhere.

On arriving at the place for my battery I found that spot had been selected because the garrison had commenced a defensive work, which would save us much labour. Ferdinand's Dyke extends from the river nearly to Merxem, affording complete cover from the artillery on the side away from the town. To remedy this, they were constructing the work, which in part now served us for a parapet, and brought us much nearer to the docks than any of the other batteries in progress.

Sub-Lieutenant Adamson had brought thither a working party of the line and made a commencement. All night our labour was incessant and unmolested by the garrison, who seemed to have had no patrols. With the dawn the interior slope of the parapet had reached its height; this was built up of sand-bags, but the upper part had not yet attained sufficient thickness to resist artillery.

Near the river, at the other extremity of the dyke, is Fort du Nord, which enfilades the whole length of the dyke. The daylight disclosed our work to the garrison, and we received several shot. The work was continued as much under cover as possible, but Sapper Northam losing his leg, and some other casualties having taken place, the men were withdrawn altogether from the exterior. The labour was now carried on under the shelter of the parapet, the men bringing the mould from the rear in baskets; thus, not advancing so rapidly, but in comparative security, the shot passing over us or lodging in the parapet. In the meanwhile, the carpenters were busy laying down the platforms for the six mortars, and an excavation was made for a powder magazine.

By noon the battery was completed, after sixteen hours' labour. Resigning it into the hands of the Artillery, I brought off the working party.

Going to the room which had been allotted to us close by the church, I found it had become a refuge for many, who sought to feel the warmth of a fire. A very acceptable bason of soup had been prepared for me, whatever it might have been in more easy times, as a principal ingredient was the rye bread. I was then sent to assist Cooper, whose battery was not completed.

Soon after three o'clock the batteries opened at the same time upon the shipping. The artillery guns consisted of a mixture of English with French and Dutch obtained in the country. Returning to the village I fell in with Hayter, who had come up recovered from the ague. The Colonel sent him to assist Capt. Thompson, who was occupied in finishing the battery for the 24-pounders, which was more exposed than the others, the French having constructed a battery in advance of the fortifications, which fired right upon it. I accompanied Hayter. The battery was in a garden near the house, and there were many trees around. We had not been long here when the scene became not a little appalling; the whiz of the shells carrying death and desolation; the crash upon the houses; the branches of the trees split and falling about. Considering our position very few suffered.

One man's escape seemed remarkable; himself thrown down, his hat knocked off by a shell, falling close and apparently touching him, who, getting up, resumed his work as if nothing had happened. Another, however, was killed, though the shot did not seem to touch him.

At dusk we accompanied Capt. Thompson to the house in which he was quartered. Being nearer Antwerp, it was much more exposed than where I was lodged with the Sappers; but it was strongly built, and belonging to a timber merchant the timber was packed upon its flat roof, affording protection. Capt. Thompson's tea was very refreshing after the fatigue of the night and day.

34

In returning to our abode for the night the heated shot and fusees of the shells presented a fine sight as they held their course overhead, but could not be contemplated without alarm as they dropped in our way. The range of the shot now from the fortifications extended nearly the length of the village, and converged upon the church tower, the only elevation for viewing the effect of the fire of our batteries. It was visited by all the principal officers, Prussian as well as English. Among other visitors was the Duke of Clarence.

During our absence the room by the church had become pretty well occupied. In addition to our servants two or three Sappers with their wives had found in it a more comfortable accommodation than their own afforded. A little after nine o'clock, wrapped in my cloak, I laid down upon some straw, almost too excited and fatigued to sleep. The employments and scenes of the day seemed still present, and the ears to be assailed with the variety of sounds which had been filling them.

4th Feb.—Sleep seemed scarcely to have obtained full possession of the faculties, when, before 2 a.m., I was roused to resume operations, less inclined to return to labour than when I laid down, and with an increased feeling of weariness.

My orders were to take a working party to make some splinter-proofs for the picquets or advanced sentinels, and to give some additional protection to the 24-pounder battery. The splinter-proofs were formed by throwing up earth against the walls of outbuildings on the side towards the town, and laying sloping beams of timber against the other side; thus a place of tolerable security was obtained.

On entering an outhouse with this object, the first thing that met the eyes was the sickening sight of the dead bodies of some whom I had seen fall the preceding evening. Alas, the folly of man! With respect to the battery, the parapet required strengthening and elevating, and protection on the side towards the town works, by a mound of earth.

During the night there was a cessation from firing. With the dawn of the morning, we discerned the French very busily employed at a new work in face of us, which appeared of a most formidable description. Our small number of guns would be able to cope but for a moment with the extended front of fire the battery presented; we were completely under their view. A very inadequate defence was scarcely accomplished. It was now eleven o'clock, when they opened fire. Our

35

gunners had taken their stations, and I withdrew the working party; it was too exposed a place to justify remaining as a spectator. The guns were quickly dismounted or rendered unserviceable.

Returning to the village, I was soon sent to take charge of the repair of some of our platforms, which had been rendered unserviceable by the firing of our own artillery. From this I returned at dusk.

Two hours later in the evening I was put in charge of a working party to make some mortar batteries along Ferdinand's Dyke in advance of our first night's battery. The place for the mortars was cut in the dyke, the mould excavated being thrown on the side towards Fort du Nord, to which we were now nearer than, before. Thus, much security was provided for the working of the mortars.

5th Feb.—Myself and working party were relieved soon after 1 a.m. Not expecting to be called upon before the morning, I ventured to undress. At four o'clock, however, I was summoned to resume the work on Ferdinand's Dyke, and having completed it before noon, the working party was brought to the village.

I found our quarters transferred to a more distant part of the village, our former abode having become untenable from the shells directed to the neighbourhood of the church. Here a smaller room served for the accommodation of us all, that is the subalterns. Abbey now joined us; he had been detained in the rear by a kick from a horse. The orders were now received through him.

In the evening it was reported that we were to retire, as we no longer could have the protection of the Prussians, Bülow being ordered to join Blücher, who, with the main army, was advancing upon Paris. We had indeed no object in remaining, having nearly exhausted the little means we possessed, and which had been found quite inadequate, for any effect produced by the fire of the artillery, however well directed, was easily arrested.

At eight o'clock in the evening took charge of a party to collect the tools and light materials from the different batteries, to have them packed in the waggons ready for moving. This was accomplished soon after midnight, and I laid myself down.

6th Feb,—We were under orders for marching this morning at five o'clock for Braeschaet. As some of the Dutch drivers had absconded with their horses, it occasioned the burning of the contents of some of the waggons. On reaching our destination, we found the village so crowded that some time elapsed before a vacant place could be obtained. Having at last taken possession of a room, we were glad to get some breakfast. Two Dutch Engineer officers who had deserted from the French increased our party.

Accommodation was so scanty, that late in the evening we heard some soldiers had taken possession of the stables allotted to our horses, which were found tied to some trees. Shelter was however obtained for them elsewhere.

7th Feb.—Marched with stores and company under Captain Thompson to Westwesel. Our billet is at the post-house in the main road, some little distance from the village, for the convenience of the waggons. Here we occupy the large receiving room of the house, in the centre of which is a great stove, which, besides keeping us warm this cold weather, answers a variety of useful purposes.

I have much to thank God for, in my preservation before Antwerp, and that my health has not suffered, notwithstanding little rest, much privation, and fatigue.

You may like to see the following extract from the General Orders of the 6th:—

It must have been evident to the whole army that the commanding officers, R.A., Sir G. Wood, and of R.E. Lieutenant-Colonel Carmichael Smyth, with all the officers and men of their respective corps, deserve the highest praise; there never was any occasion when better arrangements for the ready execution of the service, or greater exertions in the course of it, were made by those distinguished corps. The want of success can only be attributed to the want of time and of greater means.

9th Feb,—We have enjoyed our rest here. Today Abbey and Cooper left us. We move to Rosendaal tomorrow. This letter is dispatched today.

Yours, &c.,   J. S.

10th Feb,—We were early on our way to replace the contents of our waggons in their former depot. As there had been a sudden thaw, and the previous day wet, the road was not so pleasant. Arriving at Rosendaal, Hayter and I obtained a very comfortable billet on an apothecary.

11th Feb.—Received your letter dated 19th Jan. Our little army is now in cantonments; Headquarters at Groot Zundert. The French are busily engaged intrenching Marxem.

12th.—The frost has returned. Engaged in the unpleasant duty of a court-martial. Several of the men had been guilty of excesses, but on account of the good conduct of the others, the colonel had passed over their faults, hoping by leniency to draw them to the path of duty. No such effect having been produced, it was thought needful to make an example of an old offender. The prisoner was found guilty of drunkenness, and being absent from his post as sentinel. The sentence was heavy, three hundred lashes.

13th Feb.—Another court-martial on a man who had forcibly attempted to extort money from an inhabitant, selling the tools, and otherwise misconducting himself, and passing himself under a feigned name. His sentence, 300 lashes with six months' imprisonment. This is the most ill-conducted man of the company.

15th Feb.—This morning we had the unpleasant duty of carrying out the sentences of the court on the two men. Being now at comparative rest, reports of all descriptions float about. It is, however, a time which gives scope for speculation, when events under the guidance of the Almighty seem to have brought the armies of great nations to a crisis. The result seems at hand, when peace shall take the place of fierce contention. A time of rejoicing to most, when, in the good providence of God, we may shortly see the sword returned to its scabbard.

To my dear brother's enquiry as to the sentiments of the people with respect to the English, I may say we are very popular in comparison of the French and Germans on account of their great exactions; but though they look upon us as their deliverers, yet a foreign army subjects them to so many inconveniences and annoyances that our presence can only be a choice of evils. To the Dutch, the French are very hateful, not only for their exactions, but also for the conscription, which breaks up their families for a service only tending to strengthen their chains. In Holland itself, there seems but one heart in the cause of liberty; nearer the borders of France the feeling is more mixed.

20th, Sunday,—We had an opportunity of attending prayers, the first Sunday we have been so favoured. The service was conducted by Mr. James, the chaplain to the forces. He shows great earnestness, and has a clear, loud, and strong voice. It was a great pleasure to hear him. His sermon was very short and to the purpose. He has to perform service at the several cantonments.

Swearing was the main subject of his sermon—a most needful one amongst us. He addressed both the officers and men in a very striking manner:

I speak to officers as well as to the men. It is not the command of a company, or a regiment, that exempts a man from responsibility to the law of God, no, nor is the general of an army, &c.

Received instructions to go to Tholen on the morrow to make a plan, and report on the fortifications, and to complete the *tête du pont* for the protection of the ferry.

21st February,—Left this morning the quiet quarters at Rosendaal, where we had passed ten days very pleasantly. Hayter, though able to go through his duties, seems very weak. This country does not suit him; when a thaw comes he will fail.

It was a fine frosty morning. Crossing the river was attended with difficulty from the floating ice. Finding the house disengaged where I had before found so kind a welcome, I got my billet on it. The old lady gave me a pleasant welcome. Reported myself to the *commandant*, Colonel Henry, who was sitting before a high-piled turf fire. Joined the artillery officers stationed here, at their dinner.

22nd February.—Employed making a sketch of the *tête du pont*, collecting bills for work done under the superintendence of Eyre, and finding contractors for new works.

27th February,—My sketch was finished on the 23rd, and sent off to Colonel Smyth. The following days were employed making observations on the fortifications for a plan and report of the defences of Tholen, which, being completed, I am sending it off to headquarters, and with it I take the opportunity of forwarding this letter.

J. S.

7

Tholen, March 3, 1814.

Received yours, My dear Father, of the 16th February, this day, for which many thanks. I have now nothing in hand but a small defensive work to protect the ferry on the Bergen-op-Zoom side of the river. The frost left us yesterday, which makes the country not so pleasant, the roads being so bad.

Rosendaal, March 10.

I resume my letter, my dearest father and mother, to ask you to join with me in praising God. Bless the Lord, our souls, and all that is within us bless His holy name; who redeemed my life from destruction. Surely God has been my refuge and fortress, His truth my shield and buckler. He hath delivered me from terror by night, and the arrow that flieth by day.

7th March,—I received an order to go to Halteren, a village between Tholen and Bergen-op-Zoom. I rode over, and found there eight sappers with two waggons of tools. As the village was full of soldiers, a billet could only be obtained at some distance. I passed the night at Tholen.

8th March.—Left early for Halteren, with the kind expression of my hostess to come to her house should I again visit Tholen. My billet at Halteren was at a cottage, the owner half labourer, half farmer. It afforded only one sitting-room for all the family, our two selves and two Dutch waggoners. How we should sleep was a question; but, as it proved, there was no occasion for taking thought for a sleeping place. As often the case, we busy ourselves in vain.

From the number of soldiers collected together in the village, as the day advanced, it became apparent that something was in view, though the particular object remained concealed, and became a subject of discussion and conjecture among the various assembled groups.

ATTACK ON BERGEN-OP-ZOOM.

Between six and seven o'clock I received a message to come to Major-General Skerret's, where his staff and a party of officers, among whom was Sir G. Hoste, were finishing dinner. He had been sent over from headquarters with instructions for an attack that night upon the fortress of Bergen-op-Zoom, which he had communicated to the general.

He now entered more into detail with me as to my part. The object was to take the garrison by surprise; ten o'clock was named for the hour of the assault, which had been fixed in reference to the attack by the river, as it was low water at that time; otherwise, a later hour would have been in every respect preferable.

He gave me a note, which stated that I was to put myself under the orders of Colonel Carleton, who commanded that portion of the 44th Regiment with the army, to lead the storming party, entering by the river into the town.

A tracing was shown me of the part of the fortifications where our attack was to be made. First, there was the dyke to be crossed close under a battery, which commanded its whole length. Then the

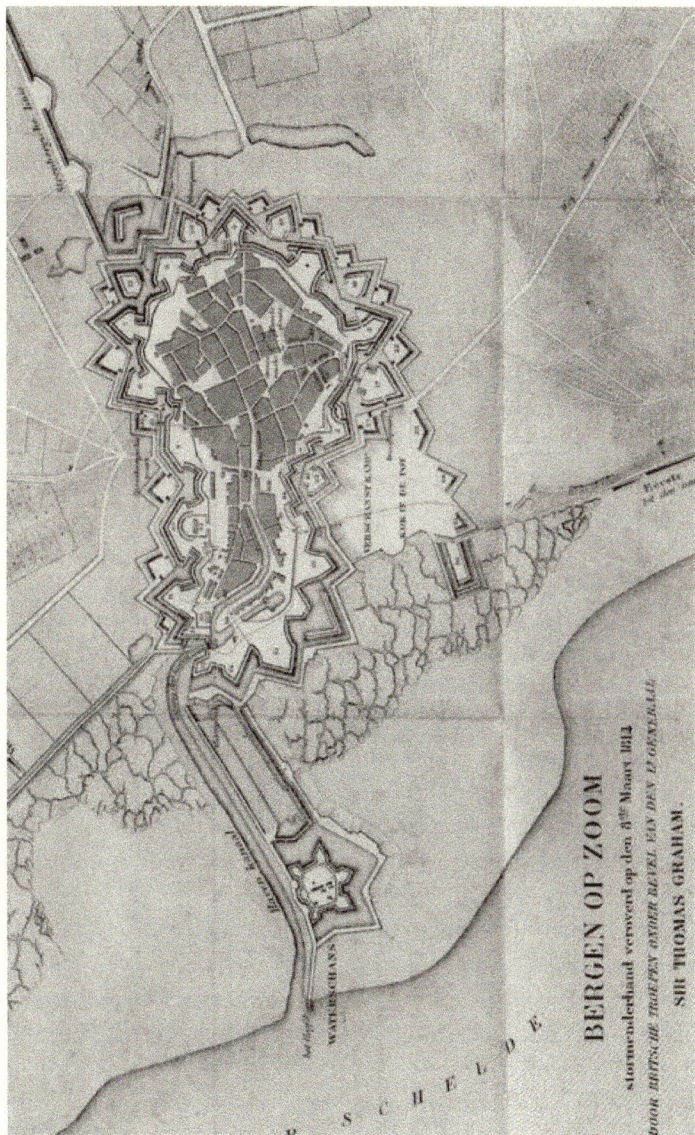

BERGEN OP ZOOM
stormenderhand verwoest op den 8sten Maart 1814
DOOR BRITSCHE TROEPEN ONDER BEVEL VAN DEN Lt-GENERAAL
SIR THOMAS GRAHAM.

descent into the river, the position of the guard-vessel in the middle of the river, with spiked harrows fixed at the bottom of the river on each side of the vessel and in front of it. The vessel itself and the entrance by the river was protected by two light pieces of artillery placed at the bend of the river into the town. These obstacles being overcome, we were to mount the right bank of the river a little beyond the guard-vessel, where stood the guardhouse. Before entering into the body of the place, there still remained some palisades to be passed, and a bridge over a curve of the river communicating with the outworks.

There were to be two other columns of attack, besides a false one to draw the attention of the garrison to the other side of the town.

Sir G. Hoste then left for his own post, as attached to Major-General Cooke, commanding one of the columns.

Bergen-op-Zoom is strongly fortified; the garrison, however, was weak and inadequate for the extensive works to be defended. The severe frost which had set in rendered it the more assailable as the wet ditches were frozen over. The ice was kept broken in the middle of the ditches; the breadth broken was not sufficient, but that by planks laid across an easy passage might be effected.

The possession of Bergen was an object to the Dutch for the defence of Holland in case of any reverse to the allies, and also affording us a ready communication with the sea. It was now a great annoyance, requiring a constant watch to prevent the garrison supplying their need by plundering the farms around.

The attack by the Water-Gate, as the more difficult and dangerous, had been committed to Carleton, who had distinguished himself on similar occasions in the Spanish sieges.

Our column was ordered to assemble at nine o'clock; the intervening time afforded an opportunity for prayer and recollection. Where so many dangers were to be encountered, hope could scarcely dare to realise an earthly existence beyond that night. It was hid in the counsels of Divine Providence who should be preserved amidst the arrows of death; and to the Almighty Director of all events I sought to commit myself, not without, I hope, a trust that whether for life or death my Redeemer liveth.

At the appointed hour we were paraded to the number of 11,000 men under the command of Major-General Skerret and Brigadier-General Gore. The Royals numbered 600; 44th, 300; two companies of 27th and 28th, 200. A selection was then made for the advanced party, or forlorn hope, who were placed under Carleton. My place was with this party with seventeen sappers, furnished with various tools and implements for clearing away palisades or other impediments to our progress. We walked in front taking the lead with the guide, who was given in special charge to two men never to lose sight of him.

Halteren, the village from whence we started, is about two miles distant from the town. The first part of the way lay along the road, from which we deviated to an open field track, the fields being separated from each other by water ditches. It was a clear bright night, and the snow, which slightly covered the ground, made our column the more distinguishable. There was nothing now to conceal us from the observation of the sentinels on the ramparts had they been on the lookout.

★★★★★★★★★★

A second column under Major-General Cooke of 1,000 men, comprising Guards and others, were to enter about Bastion 4 from the Water Gate, and two from the Antwerp Gate.

A third column of 1,200 were to have entered near the Breda Gate, but finding the garrison lining the ramparts, as they were late, followed to the place where the Guards entered. Thus, there would be about 3,000 men in Bergen-op-Zoom, a much larger number than the garrison. Some of the false attack made good an entrance.

1st column, Major-General Skerret	11,000
2nd do. Major-General Cooke	1,000
3rd do.	2,100
False attack	650

★★★★★★★★★★

It was an anxious time as we wended our way in this exposed situation to the dyke, which preserves these lands from the inundation of the river. The barking of a dog greatly alarmed us, and this followed by a musket going off accidentally in the rear quickened our apprehensions lest discovery should entirely frustrate the object of our expedition. A complete surprise could only give a prospect of success to an attack like ours upon a place so carefully prepared with every means of defence.

At last, the dyke was reached, and we commenced filing along it to the fortifications, having in our face the battery which swept the whole length of the dyke on both sides. What a position was this to be in! Happily, we were unperceived.

We now arrived close under the ramparts, and halted in anxious suspense for ten o'clock before crossing the dyke and descending into the river.

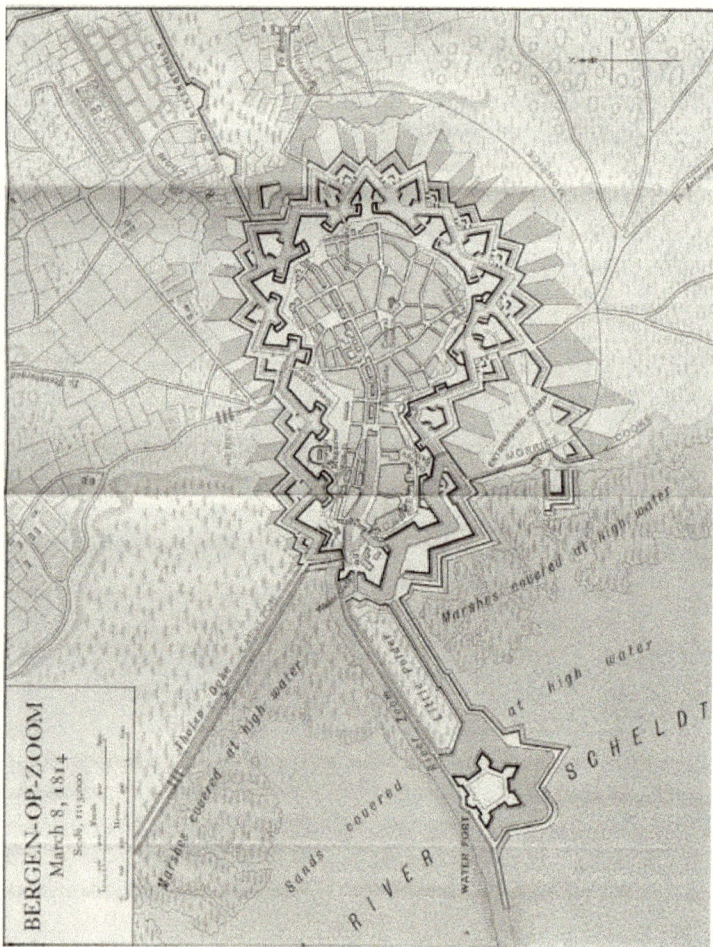

BERGEN-OP-ZOOM
March 8, 1814
Scale 1/13,000

PLAN OF THE ASSAULT

It was barely ten when the sound of distant firing reached us. The alarm was thus given. There was no time to be lost. We scrambled up as well as we could the slippery sides of the dyke. The battery opened its fire, accompanied with one of small arms. Our safety consisted in rushing forward. As we jumped into the river, the guard, panic-struck, and ignorant of the extent of danger, hurried out of the vessel, and we, getting through the spikes and water, followed its defenders up the river. I was a little in advance of the colonel, who, turning suddenly to the right, got up its bank, crying out, "I am in first."

We hastened to the guard-house, which was almost deserted, the men being occupied upon the ramparts firing at our people who were crossing the dyke. They made little defence, and gave up their arms, bewildered by the suddenness and boldness of the attack. The officer of the guard surrendered his sword to me.

Having disarmed the guard, we took them with us. Our party consisted only of the advance. Those following were checked, and left the advance unsupported on account of the fire from the other side of the river. We now proceeded to the palisades, which presented no obstacle, the gate having been left open. The bridge over the river, which formed the communication between the town and outworks, was not drawn up, thus affording a free passage. Here, according to our instructions, we took to the right hand along the ramparts.

General Gore agreed with Carleton that it was better not to pause for the rest of the column, but to advance rapidly, to prevent the rallying of the different guards, and with the prospect of meeting General Cooke's column.

In our progress along the rampart at first, we only fell in with the sentries, and then larger parties. They were all disarmed, the muskets being thrown over the rampart into the ditch, and the prisoners following in the rear.

We came to a halt about the fourth bastion, disappointed as to meeting General Cooke's column, of the place of whose entry, by some oversight, we had not been informed, though we were now near the very spot; but they were very late. Our bugle was sounded, but in vain we listened for any response. I do not think our party exceeded one hundred and fifty—probably under. Our prisoners were, however, more numerous, which in the dusk gave some importance to our body.

Again, we resumed our progress along the ramparts, to prevent the assemblage of our opponents. It was found it did not answer to stand

45

to fire, as our adversaries did the same; but when we ran upon them, they either surrendered or made their escape down the slopes. Our men, however, could not be kept from firing, which in the darkness was dangerous to ourselves. The colonel complained of being separated from his own men, and being placed over others who neither knew him nor his voice.

We had now advanced more than half round the ramparts, and were quite at a loss to account for not having seen or heard anything of the other attacking columns so anxiously looked for. We had passed the Antwerp, and were close upon the Breda Gate. At Bastion No. 8 our progress was arrested by a more numerous body than we had hitherto encountered, who seemed determined to contest our further advance. This bastion was planted with trees, from behind which they fired upon us. Our party returned the fire. Their ardour being damped, were reluctant to come to the charge.

We had, however, become mixed with them in hand to hand fight around the trees, and were making prisoners, when the slow beat of a drum attracted our attention. As this ominous sound drew nearer, our opponents took fresh courage, while it filled us with anxiety. We soon discerned a large body of men advancing with measured step along the curtain leading to the bastion in which we were engaged. Our contest was renewed with fresh energy.

A ball felled General Gore, which I noticed to Colonel Carleton. The column still gradually and cautiously approached, with the same ominous beat of drum, until they had entered to the middle of the bastion, when they came to a halt, as if to discern between friends and foes.

This gave our brave colonel an opportunity of rallying his little band, and the prisoners in our rear concealed in some measure the insignificance of our numbers. Observing their hesitation (for a sort of solemn pause had taken place), our gallant colonel put on a bold face, and, stepping in advance, said, "*Messieurs, mettez bas vos armes.*" The answer was a volley of musketry, and this distinguished officer fell to the ground.

Our party now made a simultaneous movement in retreat, but finding that after a little firing the column resumed its former caution, with slow step and beat of drum, we retired leisurely, with the hope of falling in with our own people. This cautious advance and hesitation of the main body of the garrison proceeded probably from the supposition that we were merely a detachment preceding the main body. It, however, proved our safety, and enabled us to bring off our prisoners, as we met with no opposition, except from stragglers who had resorted to the ramparts.

When we had retired to about the place where the advance had been sounded in our previous progress, we discerned a large body of men in front of us. We anxiously hailed them. They, knowing that no column had entered in the direction from which we came, had so entirely concluded us enemies, and were prepared to treat us as such, that no response was made to our cry.

Imagine our mutual joy when we recognised each other, and found that this was Major-General Cooke's column, consisting principally of the Guards, which had effected its entrance by the *bâtardeau*. The other column, which attempted an entrance near the Breda Gate, the next bastion to the one where we met our repulse, had been obliged to retire with considerable loss, and were brought in following the Guards.

With General Cooke I had the pleasure of falling in with Colonel Smyth and Sir G. Hoste, and exchanging mutual congratulations, considering that the place was ours; but was sorry to hear that Abbey was shot through the leg and arm (he now lies in a doubtful state), and Adamson killed by a shot through the head.

The opinion of our leaders was that we should remain quiet during the night, and take possession in the morning. Colonel Smyth then took his leave to report to the general, Sir G. Hoste accompanying him.

The plan adopted seemed unhappy. Here we were, men and officers standing about in a cold night. There were some casements or damp vaults where we passed some of the time. Close to the ramparts ran the wall of a garden, where was a small building, but carried up as a sort of look-out or summer-house, much higher than the surrounding houses, so as to give a commanding view. Here the general took up his abode.

Our passiveness was misconstrued, and invited attack. The garrison got possession of the houses of the streets abutting upon the ramparts, and annoyed us greatly. A sharp contest ensued, and they were driven out. Bullets were continually whizzing round us during the night.

From our quietness the garrison began to resume courage, and make little attacks. They retired immediately on our men showing themselves, but these not following up their assailants, it only encouraged a repetition of them. Allowing them to be the aggressors revived their hopes.

The Attack on Bergen-op-Zoom

Believing myself the only Engineer officer in the place, I made frequent visits to the look-out, to see if the general had any orders. Lord Proby, who commanded the Guards, was filled with melancholy forebodings. He had taken up his post with the general, and seemed occupied in instilling the diffidence with which his own mind was filled. He characterized our situation as desperate, (although exactly the reverse, as any decisive measure must, humanly speaking, have insured success,) and the importance of the safety of the Guards.

Our position as the morning dawned was about as follows:—We had possession of the ramparts, from the Antwerp Gate to the Waterport, with the interruption of occasional stragglers, and probably as much further as we had chosen to send any party in force. That part of General Skerret's column which had been checked by the fire from the ramparts, and had not followed the advance, had turned to the left-hand rampart, of which they gained possession, and with it the command of the arsenal. The general, however, had been killed.

Part, also, of the false attack had established themselves near the Steinbergen Gate.

It was greatly in our favour that the inhabitants were all with us. We were much more numerous than the garrison; and though they ventured to approach us, yet the moment the infantry showed themselves they ran off.

The Royal Scots, who formed part of the Water-Gate column, seem unaccountably to have remained in the outwork, instead of following into the town, or at least a number of them. Now the outwork was entirely commanded by the town ramparts, and a party of the garrison coming thither at dawn, saw the position of the Royals, and fired upon them, who then ran to the further end of the outwork for shelter.

The general's attention was drawn to this from the look-out. Instead of a detachment being sent to drive away the stragglers who were firing upon the Royals, and when all was expectation of some decisive movement, to take possession of the place, we were surprised by an order for the Guards to leave the town.

Their colonel withdrew his men by the way they entered. The other regiments occupied the ramparts to cover their retreat. The Guards were reluctant to abandon their comrades, and many of them gave expression to their feelings in thus retiring before the French and deserting their companions.

Those that remained were quite equal to the taking of the place, had there been a leader. Seeing, however, the turn things were taking, and that a capitulation was purposed, I went to the general to ask him whether, as the sappers could be of no further service, I might withdraw them. With his consent we followed the Guards by the *bâtardeau*.

Outside the works were Sir Thos. Graham and Colonel Smyth, much cast down at the result of an undertaking which had promised so fairly. With them was a large reinforcement ready to march in. The race is not always to the swift, nor the battle to the strong. The colonel smiled at my trophy, and directed me to go to Rosendaal.

Being on the Antwerp side of the town, the river cut us off from Halteren, obliging us to make the circuit of the fortifications. The corpse of poor Adamson lay in an outhouse, and several of the wounded in a house near. Abbey had been removed to Rosendaal.

★★★★★★★★★★

It seems evident that the failure of the assault arose partly from some misunderstanding, as it respects the false attack. At ten o'clock, which was the critical moment of the assault of the different columns, when everything demanded the greatest stillness, the false attack made as much noise as they could, with firing, and brought the garrison everywhere to the ramparts. But for this, at the river we should have made our entrance almost unperceived, with an undivided column, and might alone, under the guidance of Carleton, have taken the town. Had General Cooke's column been more punctual, they would have entered harmless, under the protection of Carleton's advance.

★★★★★★★★★★

As we made our way round, a brisk firing was going on along the ramparts on this side of the fortifications; and when afterwards they heard of the capitulation, many made their escape across the ditch. We reached Halteren about noon; found my servant anxiously on the watch, and not a little relieved by my appearance.

Having collected our goods, we proceeded to Rosendaal, where I am comfortably billeted.

A bullet passed through my hat, close above my head, another through my coat. My three leading companions, Generals Skerret and Gore and Colonel Carleton, were killed; then, again, Abbey and Adamson.

May that night be always remembered with thankfulness to God, and the life which He so graciously preserved show forth His praise.

Yours, &c.,   J. S.

8

Rosendaal, 12th March, 1814.

My last was written on the 10th, about midnight. I was roused from sleep by a dragoon, with a letter from Colonel Smyth, desiring me to write an account of all that came under my own observation, from the time I joined Colonel Carleton till I left Bergen-op-Zoom, and to bring it to headquarters.

11th March,—I arose, and set to work.

In the morning took my statement over to Calmthout. There I was requested to write another copy for the general. Sir Thomas was kind enough to ask me to stay to dinner, but the colonel wished me to return to arrange for the funeral of poor Abbey, who died that morning.

A flag of truce was sent into Bergen concerning the wounded who have been brought out of Bergen. All the officers and soldiers, after being put on parole, have been sent out. They are to return to England.

Rosendaal is now accommodating the wounded officers and soldiers. After the late event there is quite a melancholy gloom. The unaccountable result of the attack is the absorbing theme.

12th March,—Colonel Smyth, with all the officers of Engineers, attended the funeral of Abbey. He was a promising officer.

In the evening Hayter unexpectedly made his appearance, quite knocked up. The climate not suiting him, and being unfit for duty, he is ordered to England on a medical certificate. Rosendaal being so crammed, I received him into my billet.

14th March.—Had received an order the preceding day to go to Tholen to see after the work left incomplete. I arrived late in the evening, and found the place occupied by the Russians. Finding my former billet unoccupied, returned to it.

Horse-shoeing in Holland is a troublesome affair, when we are separated from our own farrier. The Dutchmen are so timid that, to shoe a horse, they place him in a sort of narrow stall, which, with iron bars and chains, is enough to frighten any unaccustomed horse to get into. While shoeing, their feet are chained in such awkward positions that the animal becomes quite unruly. My horse passed through this operation today.

16th March,—Relieved by Eyre, and returned to Rosendaal. Here I found Sir George Hoste had orders for my going to Braeschaet to relieve Captain Thompson at a work going on there. As I leave in the morning, I avail myself of the present opportunity to finish this letter. Found your two letters with Hayter, waiting my return, for which I thank you.

Writing so fully to yourself, I must ask you kindly to communicate to my brothers and to Clifton when writing. Hayter is leaving for England. The long frost still continues. I have the pleasure of falling in occasionally with Pringle. He is, I understand, now on duty at Braeschaet, which will make my stay there more agreeable.

I am, &c.,   16th March, Rosendaal.

9

Entrenchment near Braeschaet,
22nd March, 1814.

My last was from Rosendaal, the eve of departure for this place to relieve Captain Thompson, who was required to settle the accounts of the prisoners going home, also in connexion with the sub-lieutenant who had been killed.

The entrenchment here consists of a large square building used as a distillery. The interior is turned into a sort of defensible barrack for the soldiers, and loopholed in case of attack.

It is situated on the high road, between Antwerp and Breda, where several roads cross. Its use is to protect our left, and to check any sorties from Antwerp. A parapet, with a ditch, has been formed round it, but of irregular shape, as the line of the garden fence has been followed. It is also palisaded, and otherwise strengthened, an adjoining wood supplying the material.

A detachment of three hundred men is furnished from the regiments near, which is daily relieved. Those not required for duty serve as a working party under the Engineer officer.

There being no accommodation in the distillery for the Artillery officers and Engineers, they had taken up their abode at a farmhouse close in the rear, which, as they are more stationary, afforded more comfort and convenience.

The dusk has set me free from the work at the entrenchment, where I have been engaged since daylight.

This being an outpost, we lay down in our clothes, to be ready on the least alarm at night. We have now beautiful sunny days, the frost leaving us, which makes the work easy and pleasant.

This afternoon I am gratified by a letter from Colonel Smyth, informing me that Captain Thompson would relieve me, and that he had appointed me Adjutant and Quartermaster to the department, *vice* Abbey.

24th March.—Captain Thompson relieved me yesterday. In the afternoon I came over to headquarters at Calmthout, and waited upon the colonel.

No billet was to be had but at a remote hovel, most unpromising without and within. Though so close upon Holland, Brabant is like a different country. The poor are all Roman Catholics, and have none of the tidy, cleanly habits of the Protestants. Potatoes, milk, and butter, with black bread, is their diet.

I entered today on my new offices, and breakfasted with the colonel. The writing, being much in arrear, confined me all day, leaving much to be done. Hayter is waiting a passage at Williamstadt. I have to thank you for a large packet of letters. Make my kind acknowledgments to the dear writers.

Yours, &c.,   25th of March.

10

29th March, Calmthout.

The poor circumstances of those on whom I am billeted only admit of their making me a sharer in their poverty. They have allotted me the second room, which is quite pervious to the wet from above. The walls are brick, and the floor was once the same. A small table and a couple of chairs have been spared to us, with some straw. There is a chimney with a hearth, which gives the comfort of a good fire, where Davis shows his cooking skill in making something out of the rations.

The paymaster is not able now to supply us with the money due to us, from the great drafts of gold to the continental subsidies.

You will like to hear something of the occupations of my new office.

There is a letter-book to keep, into which I have to copy all official letters sent or received, and others which may be of interest, as well as of useful memoranda; to enter the instructions or letters to officers concerning their different employments, or to others connected with the department. There is also the daily regimental return for the quartermaster-general; the return for the men's working pay; to get the General Orders for each day. These are all much in arrear. From this you will perceive that one of the more intelligent sappers must be trained to act as clerk.

The colonel expects me to breakfast with him, and afterwards to remain at work, according to circumstances. As adjutant and quarter-master, I receive an extra pay of three shillings per day.

26th March.—Yesterday was occupied all the day writing. Today accompanied the Colonel to Braeschaet. Meeting Sir Thos. Graham there, he kindly gave me an invitation to dinner, which was thankfully accepted. Colonel Smyth always has a seat at the general's table.

27th March.—Report of the advance of a body of French, under General Maçon. I was sent to Capt. Thompson, to discontinue the work at Braeschaet.

28th March.—Accompanied the colonel about the construction of some redoubts for the protection of Rosendaal.

29th March.—We were to have moved our headquarters this day. This has been countermanded. It seems that General Thielman, with a body of Saxons, is in pursuit of Maçon, who has collected something of an army from the different French garrisons to enable him to keep the field, to cut off the supplies going to the Allied Army.

Upon the intelligence that, instead of being reinforced, the garrison of Antwerp had been diminished, the occupation of our batteries on the Scheldt was resumed.

I was sent to Westwesel to Captain Thompson, with orders for his resuming the work at Braeschaet, in the morning.

As there is a mail leaving, I bring my letter to a conclusion, and remain, &c.,

J. S.

11

Calmthout, 2nd April, 1814.

The quickness of communication between the two countries renders our situation here much more agreeable than it otherwise might be. Three mails have arrived without a letter from you. It being part of my duty to receive and forward the letters to the officers and men at their different stations, think how eagerly I turn over the letters to find one for myself.

Colonel Smyth makes himself very kind. His billet is pleasantly situated on the village-green; my hovel at a considerable distance. As a general officer was calling today, and making a long visit, I strolled out, and was attracted by the church standing prettily among some trees at one extremity of the green. There were many cattle about; and, going to the church, by a pretty path that led to it, there were cattle alongside. On entering the church, I was surprised to find it turned into a slaughterhouse. War seems to place itself above all respect for days, times, or places.

It is a Roman Catholic church, and, as they generally are, adorned with pictures, trinkets, and other ornaments. What a contrast it presented to a place of worship! In one part they were killing a beast, in another skinning one just killed; a little beyond cutting up into joints, and then again weighing the several pieces, and delivering them to the parties waiting to be supplied. The pavement flowed with, blood. I need not say it was a distressing sight. The path leading to the church was lined with beasts waiting their turn for the butcher's stroke.

Through the Swedish headquarters Sir Thomas received a letter this morning announcing the victory of the allies. A *feu de joie* has been fired in consequence. Two additional captains of Engineers have joined us, Oldfield and Harris.

3rd April.—The colonel wished me to accompany him on an excursion to the gates of Bergen-op-Zoom to ascertain the best position for the construction of some small redoubts, more effectually to confine the garrison. Having some distance to go to get my horse, I found on my return that he had started for Rosendaal, to get from thence the officers who were to be entrusted with the execution of the different works.

Having at length ascertained his route, it seemed better to return to Rosendaal, where we were to lodge for the night, which I reached about dusk, but the colonel did not appear till nearly nine in the evening.

I was billeted in the same house with the colonel; it was a house of good size and appearance, containing a large family. We sat down a numerous party to supper. Our hosts were Roman Catholics, and, being Friday, it was remarkable the number of nice dishes which covered the table without any recourse to animal food.

4th April.—We left our pleasant abode after breakfast, going to the Wouw and Antwerp Gates of Bergen, on the roads leading to which the colonel gave directions for the construction of redoubts. We returned to Calmthout, passing through some very pretty country, consisting of sandhills wooded with fir, interspersed with pieces of water.

On our arrival we heard of the surrender of Paris to the Allies.

8th April.—With the exception of a visit to Braeschaet, principally employed in writing since the 4th. This morning we had the Emperor of Russia's proclamation at Paris. It seems strange at such a moment we should be making arrangements for the siege of Fort Batz, a strong fort which commands the navigation of the Scheldt. It has a garrison of a thousand men.

With the exception of the marines now in the island the rest of the force will assemble at Tholen, to the number of 1,600, under the command of General Gibbs. Colonel Smyth talks of going for a few days. Two captains and three lieutenants of Engineers are under orders.

Yours, &c.,   8th April.

12

Calmthout, 12th April, 1814.

My dearest Father,

In the magnitude of the events which have been taking place in connexion with the movements of the Allied Armies on Paris, and the consequent transactions now resulting there which absorb general attention, Holland must be forgotten. It is, however, my pleasure to feel that a communication from this corner will have its interest to the loved ones to whom I write.

My last letter left this on the 8th. The following day, 9th April, the colonel took me with him to breakfast with Sir Thos. Graham. I had the pleasure also of receiving a letter from you.

In our way to Tholen we rode partly round Bergen, approaching as near as we could with safety. We visited also the redoubts in progress of construction near the gates.

On arriving at Tholen we found there the other officers of Engineers. The town, from the passage of the troops to South Beveland, was very much crowded, having, in addition, the Russian garrison. After several unsuccessful attempts to realise a billet, I had recourse to my old friend the widow, who kindly received me to her own inconvenience, as three officers were already quartered upon her house.

10th April, Sunday,—The troops, with the stores, sailed to Yerseke, South Beveland. As Colonel S. only intended going over for so short a time, I left the horses, with the baggage not needed, at Tholen. We sailed in a Dutch *skuyt*.

Yerseke is a very neat little town. Here I was billeted; so also, the other officers intending to march early next morning.

Great part of the stores were packed in waggons ready for moving towards Batz. We went to rest, under the impression that the following night we should be constructing trenches and batteries.

11th April.—With the morning, however, came joyful tidings that Bonaparte had abdicated, and that an armistice had been concluded.

A stop was put to our proceedings. The news became the general subject of conversation. The colonel directed me to make a general survey of the town, with a plan.

A flag of truce was sent into the fortress of Batz, and an armistice concluded.

Before the intelligence arrived, some of our troops had made a forward movement to drive in the garrison picquets; from this, by the cannon of the fort, some few casualties had taken place.

The intelligence, however, arrived very providentially; a day later we should most likely have lost many lives in the first dangerous operations of a siege. One could not help feeling grateful to God for the timely interposition, as in the attack of so strong and well-armed a fort as Batz, many lives must have been sacrificed.

In the afternoon I returned with Colonel S. to Tholen. There we found the news was not at all credited. No official report had been received. Their unbelief made a little impression upon us.

12th April.—In the night there was an alarm that the French were attacking the town from Bergen. There was a general beat to arms. It, however, proved to be nothing.

In the morning, as we rode by Bergen to Calmthout, we learnt that the garrison had made a sortie to ascertain what we were about with our redoubts. Fire-balls and rockets had been thrown to give light, apprehensive that we were constructing batteries.

When we reached headquarters in the afternoon, the intelligence was abundantly confirmed.

What gratitude ought it to excite in all our hearts for so glorious a termination of the war. Indeed, what has taken place in the last year appears astonishing. The more one considers, the more wonderful do the dealings of the Almighty seem. He lifteth up and He casteth down. May our trust be in Him!

14th April.—Rode over to Oudenbosch and Rosendaal to arrange about the removal of some of our men, as the Dutch troops are about to occupy Rosendaal.

Carnot, the French Governor of Antwerp, and of their possessions in these parts, is not at all satisfied with the Paris negotiations. He has published orders, talking a great deal about the disgrace of France. He wants to have five miles round Antwerp and Bergen, to which. Sir Thomas not agreeing, no armistice is concluded. We have now 26,000 Dutch troops. Headquarters are to be moved. Left upon Lier, and right upon Braeschaet. Headquarters will be in an intermediate village. It does not now appear so improbable but that we may soon have the happiness of meeting to unite in praising God for His mercies.

J. S.

13

Headquarters, S. Graven Wesel,
18th April, 1814.

Headquarters changed today, and our force has taken up its new position. A change of quarters from Calmthout was on every account desirable, from the deficiency of the accommodation. I speak, however, in special reference to myself. My health was beginning to suffer from the damp bricks. The numbers of crickets chirping about what I cannot call a hearth, with other insects nurtured in the dirt, absence of all furniture and utensils, make the change very welcome. Not that I would in anywise complain, but rather gratefully enhance the comforts of my present position: a house not pervious to every shower, but attractive in every respect. At Calmthout, however, Marlborough had his headquarters for a short time.

The village of S. Graven Wesel is well adapted for us. It affords a handsome *château* for headquarters, and other good houses for the heads of departments.

I am in the same house with Colonel Smyth. It is the residence of the *curé* of the parish, and affords to each a bedroom, also a large sitting-room, which the colonel makes common to us both. There is a garden to the house, which is now bursting forth, making the residence very pleasant. We have had some delightful weather, and the last two days gentle rains, giving life to the vegetable world.

It is reported that the white cockade was adopted yesterday in Antwerp. We have no regular communication with the town yet. Some of the regiments here, with the Rocket Brigade, have received orders for America.

21st April.—Everything is quiet. The general is going to Brussels. The colonel accompanies him. On his return proposes a visit to the Hague and Amsterdam. I shall of course be tied down here, but have everything to make me comfortable and thankful.

****

In 1805, Captain Carmichael Smyth accompanied, as Commanding Engineer, the expedition under Sir David Baird for the recapture of the Cape of Good Hope.

After the defeat of the Dutch and the surrender of Cape Town, Captain Smyth acted there as Colonial Secretary until 1808, when he returned with Sir David Baird to England, and with him joined Sir John Moore's expedition to Spain.

This accounts for his familiarity with the Dutch language.

****

The colonel, who speaks Dutch very well, and is familiar with the language, has a grammar and dictionary, of which I am availing myself to learn the language. As the mail leaves sooner on account of the general's departure, not to lose the opportunity, I bring my letter to a close. Do not trouble yourself about the newspaper, as the colonel has the daily paper by every mail, of which I have the use. Am now quite well, enjoying the delights of this beautiful spring. What a contrast to the severe winter and its work. All praise to the Gracious Author of all our mercies.

With, &c.,   J. S.

14

St. Graven Wesel,
27th April, 1814.

My dear Father,

As your letter of the 16th came under the colonel's cover, I did not get it till his return yesterday. We hear nothing of a return to England. By an armistice with Antwerp, all except the military have free ingress and egress. Exercising one of the horses this morning, my servant's curiosity tempted him into the town.

The colonel coming in from the general, brings the tidings of a Convention being signed. We take possession of Antwerp. The French quit all this part of the country. In the event of our occupying the fortified towns, work will be afforded for our officers in plans, reports, &c.

The country here, especially at this season, is not the uninteresting country you may imagine, from its flatness. It presents many agreeable points from the arrangement of the woods. The lines of dykes, ornamented with trees, have a pretty effect, affording shady rides in the heat of the day. There are a great number of gentlemen's seats or *châteaux* laid out with pleasure-grounds, gardens, and pieces of water. Some of the houses, besides the canal which encloses the grounds, are also surrounded with water, to which the only access is by a bridge to the door.

As the colonel always dines with the general, I have made an arrangement with the *curé* to dine with him, which is pleasant. We are very sociable together. Our differences often form subjects for our conversation. The hour is between two and three o'clock. Today two gentlemen from Antwerp joined us. They said the inhabitants of Antwerp were longing for the departure of the French and the entrance of the English. The Dutch, as well as the people of Brabant, prefer our being quartered upon them, rather than any other troops, or even their own countrymen, as we pay for what we have. Many of them, taking advantage of this, become extortionate. To be rid of their exactors, they may well wish us into Antwerp.

It is, however, a gratification to be so well received everywhere. At Brussels I hear from the colonel they quite rejoiced at the sight of an Englishman, looking upon us as the liberators of the Continent. The exertions of England are quite astonishing. In the hands of Dutch, Russian, German, are seen the English firelock, besides arms and accoutrements, large supplies of clothing, besides the money subsidies. The inhabitants talk of all sorts of rejoicings on our entrance into Antwerp. This is all now suppressed by the presence of the French.

29th, Mail day, with, &c., J. S.

15

S. Graven Wesel,
2nd May, 1814.

My dear Father,

Since my last, the troops have been on the move, preparatory to taking possession of the assigned fortresses to be held by us at the time appointed by the Convention. An Austrian general has been selected by the Allies to act as a commissioner, with powers from the French Government.

This morning I accompanied the commanding officers of Artillery and Engineers, with the other officers of each corps, into Antwerp. We were attended also by the heads of the different departments, with their staff. A selection was to be made of different officers to receive over the stores of their special department, in Antwerp, and the various forts occupied by the French, who, on their part, did the same, appointing officers to deliver them up. We made altogether a large cavalcade, and were welcomed by the inhabitants, who expressed their pleasure at our entrance. The town boys preceded us with loud shoutings.

We breakfasted together at the "*Grand Labourer*," the principal hotel. The landlord was not considerate in his charges. The French Commanding Engineer seemed an intelligent officer, and we had some pleasant converse. He said he would prefer defending Antwerp to any fortress in Europe. He expressed great surprise at our leaving Bergen-op-Zoom, after having it in possession. I returned with the colonel, but the other officers went to the different posts assigned them.

From the foreign subsidies our paymaster is so badly supplied with gold that for two months I have not been able to get any pay. The colonel has been kind enough to supply my temporary need, but now he is bankrupt. To get money, except through the paymaster, is attended with heavy loss from the exchange and attendant expenses.

You will be gratified with a copy of a letter from Pall-Mall, which the colonel had inserted in the orders of this day:—

Pall-Mall, 2nd April, 1814.

Sir,—Lieutenant-General Mann desires me to inform you that His Lordship, the Master-General, before whom your report of the gallant, though unsuccessful, attack upon the fortress of Bergen-op-Zoom has been laid, has expressed himself highly satisfied with the zealous conduct of yourself and the officers of Engineers, as well as the officers, non-commissioned officers, and soldiers of the Royal Sappers and Miners on the above occasion.

I am also desired to convey a particular approbation of the gallantry and ability shown by Lieutenant Sperling, while attached to the advanced party which first entered the fortress under the immediate command of the late Colonel Carleton.

You will be pleased to make known this communication to the officers and men under your orders.

I am, &c., &c.,

(Signed)   John Rowley,
          Deputy-Inspector-General of Fortifications.

16

S. Graven Wesel,
5th May, 1814.

My dear Father,

Our troops made their entry into Antwerp at an early hour this morning. They had to relieve the French from their various guards at, the different gates and at official residences connected with the town, which occupied some time. This being accomplished, the general made his entry, followed by all the staff, amid the joyous acclamations of the townspeople. Flags of various devices were suspended from the windows. Our cavalcade proceeded under these greetings to the Place du Meir, where our soldiers were assembled to the number of about 5,000. The keys of the city were then handed over to the Commissioner of the Allied Powers.

Sir Thomas then inspected the troops. Afterwards we accompanied him on horseback round the fortifications of the town and citadel, dockyard, &c.

I accompanied the colonel in a visit to the places where we had erected our batteries for the destruction of the shipping. Few vestiges of them remained, and precautions had been taken to prevent their reoccupation with safety.

The French have left in the Engineers' office many excellent plans, of which we have certified the receipt, as well as of the other stores, to be delivered up to whatever Power Antwerp may be allotted in the arrangements taking place. In the meantime, copies are to be taken of those that might prove serviceable to ourselves. With the same view it is arranged for the officers to draw up reports on all the fortresses entrusted to our keeping.

Many parts of the town and fortifications testify to the antiquity of Antwerp. There are some good streets and many excellent houses. The smaller and poorer streets are not cleansed, which takes away from the pleasantness of this city. Of the strength of the fortifications, I need say nothing. In addition to the old works, Carnot has added new ones in advance, which make the approach more difficult.

What adds so much to the strength of the fortifications in this country is the power of overflowing the land round them. Antwerp cannot be thus surrounded; but upon those parts which are above the sea level there is concentrated a power of artillery. This also gives strength to the smallest forts, as they can only be approached by the dykes, along which the fire of their guns is directed.

The colonel thinks it will be more convenient to reside in the town, on account of the office and its superintendence, so a billet has been taken to accommodate us both, which is on the magnificent house built and inhabited by the celebrated painter, Rubens. Headquarters will continue at some of the country seats, about two miles outside Antwerp, and the colonel will probably be much at the general's. Returned to Graven Wesel.

6th May.—Took leave of the *curé*, with his enjoyable garden and pleasant bowers, to remove to Antwerp. I shall regret the country; the time passed so pleasantly, after the rough scenes we had been passing through. The spring has also been delightful, and the quiet meals with the *curé* agreeable. The rooms here feel gloomy after the cheerfulness of the country, looking into a large court. These stately houses do not make the most pleasant ones. My rooms are on the ground-floor.

7th May, 1814.—I accompanied the colonel and Sir G. Hoste to Bergen-op-Zoom, to meet the general. I was made one of the party, to point out the various circumstances of the attack and the localities.

They went in a gig; I rode on horseback. Great part of the road was deep in sand. We put up at the *Cour de Hollande.* The general, with his brother, Colonel Graham, soon arrived.

We all dined together. The table-cloth damask, with the battles of the Duke of Marlborough, attracted our notice.

8th May,—We met at breakfast. Afterwards we walked round the fortifications, and about the town, which is neat and clean, but not large. Two months have passed since the attack, and our inspection only makes the result the more remarkable. The general and his brother left. We returned to Antwerp by Fort Lillo, dining together at the "*Grand Labourer.*"

10th May,—Yesterday was my first attendance at the *Hotel de Salm*, the name by which the Engineers' Office is known. It is now made the centre of our communication. Here I have to attend every morning, for the circulation of orders, and the various duties of my office.

Thanks for the letters received this morning. In the afternoon rode to headquarters, Fort du Nord, round the glacis and new works of the place.

There have been illuminations on account of the entry of the English; another on Sunday, in honour of the Pope.

On account of the number of fortresses to be occupied there has been a considerable increase in the number of Royal Engineer officers, and another company of sappers. It has been thought desirable to arrange a mess at an hotel, instead of dining, as we now do, subject to their charges. The price fixed is three *francs* a-day.

As Pringle, of the Artillery, is here, we frequently ride out together. They have no mess, so I dine with him on Sundays.

17

Middleburg, 23rd May.

My dear Father,

Yours was received on the 14th.

I have nothing of any interest for you till the 2lst. The colonel has for some time mentioned making the tour of the forts on the Scheldt, to enable him to draw up his report on the river and its defences. With his usual kindness, he made me one of a party for the excursion. A decked vessel has been engaged for the occasion. Besides ourselves, there is General Ferguson and his *aide-de-camp*, Lieutenant Duncan, and Lieut.-Colonel Jones, of the Guards.

We embarked at five in the morning. Our *schuyt* had two cabins, a larger and a smaller one. We partook of a comfortable breakfast, and landed at Liefenshock, a strong fort opposite to Lillo, which has full command of the river. Having looked over the fort, we returned to the vessel. With a fair wind, and very fine day, we reached Flushing about five o'clock.

Having arranged our quarters satisfactorily at the inn, and reported our arrival to the Dutch *commandant*, we took a walk to survey the fortifications.

Except on the sea-fronts, they are not constructed in masonry. The earthen works are strengthened by an advanced ditch. Since our attack several strong exterior forts have been built, which render the approach difficult, especially by the dykes.

Having the power of inundation, these are the only approaches, except in severe frost. The barracks are bomb-proof. Extensive works were progressing when it was given over to the Dutch. The fortifications are abundantly armed with ordnance, especially the seafront, amongst which there is one piece, between mortar and gun, of immense weight of metal, from which dispatches, enclosed in a shell, were sent over to Catsand. The town itself still bears the marks of our bombardment; and, from the loss of their trade, means have not been found for the repairs by its inhabitants.

The accommodations of the inn were very comfortable. Our *schuyt* was ordered round to Terveer, the other side of the island, from whence it was purposed to re-embark.

22nd May,—This morning the survey of the place was completed. The day had become overcast, and rain fell heavily. About mid-day we left Flushing for Middleburg, in one of the hooded conveyances of the country, between cart and carriage. Though entirely flat, the scenery was far from unpleasing, the road prettily winding among the trees

This was Sunday. The feeling that I should have no control over it had led me rather to waive the colonel's very kind invitation. My objections were, however, overruled. In all our active operations during the war, Sunday was undistinguished, and subsequently little heeded, except by an occasional service. By a few individuals it was more regarded.

Our drive was short. The *Groote Heeren Lodgement*, at Middleburg, had the appearance of a private house. It was a welcome sight to find the Sunday rest appreciated. The door was opened to receive Sunday travellers with hesitation; they hardly seemed to know what to make of so unexpected an intrusion.

After some deliberation we were admitted. As the sleeping accommodation fell short, requiring five rooms, Colonel Smyth and self were very well accommodated across the street. The inns here are as comfortable and quiet as private houses, affording very good accommodation. We had a pleasant room for our common use, and for meals.

The owners of the house where I slept were entirely of a different description to those of the hotel. The contrast was remarkable. They were playing cards. On inquiry, I found they were Roman Catholics.

23rd May.—After breakfast we were driven through the rain to Terveer, which we reached at ten o'clock, the appointed hour for the boat. The pilot, however, deemed it too rough to think of sailing. Finding Terveer, a sort of fishing town, not affording pleasant accommodation, it was decided to resume our very comfortable quarters at the *Groote Heeren* for another day, from whence I now have had the pleasure of writing thus far to you.

24th May.—The weather continuing unfavourable, we are detained at Middleburg; with respect to myself, very pleasantly. The town is remarkably clean and neat. So pretty a one I have not seen in Holland. Should the rain cease, I hope to give you a better account.

Terveer was occupied by the French, who strengthened its fortifications.

As some of our party are much interested in old books and prints, we have been ransacking the treasures which this out-of-the-way place affords. It has furnished us with very pleasant occupation during the rain. Considerable purchases have been made from tempting portfolios.

In the afternoon, the rain ceasing, we had an opportunity of walking through the town, still decorated with triumphal arches and garlands, testifying to the joy of being liberated from the bondage in which they have so long been held.

We ascended the church tower, which has a commanding and interesting view of the town and island.

There is something very pleasing in the appearance of a Dutch town from the extreme attention to cleanliness and propriety, and particularly so when the buildings are of a description to contribute to the general effect produced by the picturesque gables of the houses.

The discordant materials of which our party is composed gave rise to many animated discussions. The mutual intercourse is, however, very pleasant and friendly. General Ferguson and Colonel Jones seem very much to differ in character, though a similarity of political opinions, strongly in opposition, has brought them together, to the surprise of many. The general appears all gentleness and kindness, while the other, both in person and manner, presents quite a contrast. Under, however, this rude exterior may be concealed softer feelings. Colonel Smyth's politics are quite a contrast.

25th May.—The delay at Middleburg has been probably more agreeable to me than to those who had calls elsewhere.

There are still the remains of the old ditch and rampart, which forms a pleasant walk round the town.

This morning we left our pleasant quarters for Terveer, the northern part of the Island of Walcheren, from which we sailed to Bergen-op-Zoom, the general being desirous of seeing the fortifications and places of attack. The rain, however, did not permit our going out this afternoon.

26th May.—General Ferguson being pressed for time, after going round the fortifications this morning, left with his party, taking a carriage for Antwerp. The colonel having to inspect Fort Batz, we remained at Bergen.

I took a more leisurely survey of the works, which, though a pattern as to their formation, are in a state of dilapidation. Examining the interior of the bastion, which was the limit of the advance of the forlorn hope, where General Gore and Colonel Carleton fell, further progress being arrested by the main body of the garrison, I found the trunks of the trees covered with the marks of the French bullets. It is a marvel that the slaughter was not greater. May I not forget my mercies!

We dined with Major von Gorcum, of the Dutch Staff, who, for the present, is stationed here, with his family. He was a captain in the French Engineers, and, being a very intelligent officer, was employed by them in the survey of Holland. He deserted to us from Antwerp, not choosing to fight against his country. He left a letter for the governor, giving his reasons for the step he had taken, stating that he had left all his plans, and should not give any information respecting a place with which he was so well acquainted as Antwerp. He was thus thrown much with the colonel, as Commanding Engineer. Also, he was with the column of Guards at the attack of Bergen. Being with some who surrendered, he, to avoid being taken, made a leap into the ditch, and so escaped.

27th May.—Early this morning we sailed from Bergen, reaching Batz after a passage of over four hours.

By the multiplication of their batteries, the French were making any aggressive approach by the Scheldt to Antwerp almost impracticable.

We looked at the fortifications of Batz with the more interest as we had been so mercifully spared its projected attack. Being considered a most important post, as the key of both the channels of the river, much care was being bestowed to add to its defences. As we now found them, they would have greatly assisted us in our attack, as, from being unfinished, they would have afforded us shelter from the fire of the fort.

With the turning tide we sailed for Antwerp, which we reached about 9 in the evening. The town, with its churches, buildings, and shipping, formed a beautiful object as we approached, illuminated by the rays of the setting sun.

30th May.—There seems a probability that I may shortly have the pleasure of seeing you all, as being the bearer of some maps and plans of importance to England.

Yours,

J. S.

18

7th June, 1814.—Since our return to Antwerp we had been going on quietly. The routine of the day was breakfast with the colonel, to take orders. Thence to the office for writing or plan-drawing, except it was a field day, or other duty. In the afternoon, generally rode into the country with Pringle, R.A., or Cooper, who shows a mind alive to the importance of religion, and under its impressions.

Maps and plans to be sent to England were deemed of sufficient importance to require an officer to take charge of them. The colonel, with his usual kindness, entrusted them to my care, and thus an opportunity was afforded me of visiting home.

I left Antwerp in the middle of the day, reaching Ghent in the evening, continuing my journey through the night; Ostend at 7 in the morning of the 8th June. The packet was to sail at 2 o'clock, but the wind did not permit. Later in the day Sir Thomas Graham (now Lord Lynedock) arrived. Also, the colonel, with Cooper, who was making the tour of the fortresses.

9th June.—Left about 4 o'clock this morning in the Harwich packet, which port not being able to make, sailed for the river, reaching Gravesend early in the morning of the 10th June. On landing, about 7 o'clock, a coach was passing into which I got, as my packages could be conveniently accommodated. At 10 o'clock my charge was delivered up at the Ordnance Office, Pall Mall. In the evening, through a merciful, gracious Providence, I was at home with loved relatives.

July 1st.—Received orders from Pall Mall to go to Woolwich, there to embark for my return to Antwerp. My stay in England had been pleasantly prolonged to wait for a transport which was being fitted up to carry out a company of sappers and some Engineer officers. It was proposed at that time to destroy the fortifications of Antwerp. This company was going out for that object, and the vessel was laden with all that was necessary for it.

19

Royal Arsenal, Woolwich,
6th July, 1814.

My dear Father,

Having the opportunity, I send my history. The time of sailing is still uncertain. On taking leave of you I called in Pall Mall. Arriving here, the luggage was sent on board, expecting to sail the next day.

I dined and slept at the rooms of my very kind academy friends, Dr. and Mrs. Parker, in the hospital. Colonel Oliver was staying with them, so I had the pleasure of again meeting one who had been so friendly in former days. Colonel and Mrs. Foy came in the evening.

As Dr. and Mrs. Parker, with Major Oliver, had arranged to spend the next day, Sunday, at her father's, Mr. Simon's, Rectory, at Paul's Cray, the Foys' most kindly pressed me to take up my abode in their house, under whose hospitable roof I still remain. The sappers went on board the transport this afternoon. On the 4th, as there were still deficiencies in the required stores, the master had to make a visit to the Tower.

The *Nelson* was launched today, of which we had a full view from the transport.

Colonel Foy gave me the pleasure of meeting at dinner Major and Mrs. Gardner, with two other ladies. In the evening Colonel Oliver, Dr. and Mrs. Parker, Captain and Mrs. Maitland, made an agreeable addition to our party. It was pleasant meeting so many old friends.

5th July,—My kind friend Colonel Handfield called this morning. He had come from town yesterday evening and was staying with General Burn, of the marines, with whom I had spent so many pleasant Sunday afternoons while at the Royal Military Academy.

At 10 p.m. I went to the transport to sleep, expecting to sail soon after midnight.

Yours, &c.,   J. S.

20

Brussels, July 11th, 1814,

My dear Father,

I was at Captain Maitland's when I was informed that there were orders for sailing.

Early the morning of the 6th we weighed anchor, and at five in the afternoon anchored off Margate, waiting till the tide would enable us to pass the breakers. Our party in the cabin consisted of five officers of engineers, one of artillery, a sub-lieutenant, with a wife and two children.

We left Margate about eight in the evening, arriving at Ostend about five the following afternoon, after a pleasant passage.

I did not stay long at Ostend, and reached Bruges about nine in the evening. At the inn where I put up there was one of our officers, who is engaged in making a plan of the place.

8th July.—Left Bruges at five in the morning. The crops in this country look amazingly well. The cultivation much attended to. Passing through Ghent, reached Antwerp in the afternoon. Colonel Smyth had, however, left the day before for Brussels. In the evening I met the other officers stationed here at Captain and Mrs. Oldfield's.

9th July,—Having to set off for Brussels, I went to seek after my horses. Found they had been removed, and placed amongst the artillery draught horses. One was laid up by a kick, the other had been bitten on the nose. Pringle breakfasted with me.

After making arrangements for changing my quarters, I mounted for Brussels. The weather is now extremely hot; the horse-flies exceedingly troublesome; and, as I took the turf road between the canal and the wood, they almost covered the poor beast. I put up at the *Hotel d'Angleterre,* whence, after dining, walked up to the colonel's quarters in the Park, but met him coming down into the town to the house of a gentleman who had with much pains collected a sort of museum, containing various objects of curiosity, where also would be assembled many amateur musicians, holding a sort of concert. I thankfully accepted the invitation to accompany him.

On entering, we found a large party of musicians, engaged with their various musical instruments, assembled in the court, over whom our host was presiding. After making the inspection of his varied collections, we walked into the garden, which was not a large one. On one side was a long building, something like our greenhouse. On its exterior were skeletons of various animals. The interior was remarkable from having each side adorned with rows of crows, with extended wings, nailed upon the walls at regular distances, but close together. The intermediate spaces were occupied by sparrows, extended in a similar manner. The lesser spaces, again, with the skulls of sparrows. The building itself contained little but the various implements used for taking the birds, which were stated to have been all caught in his own garden, though in the midst of the town.

He appears a young man, and, perhaps, the greatest of all his curiosities.

Several officers were present. While the concert was proceeding, and various pieces played, the museum afforded a diversion.

The colonel expressed himself pleased at my return, but mentioned that he had written that my coming back might not be hurried.

11th July,—I had purposed returning to Antwerp today, but the colonel thinks it better to remain till tomorrow. Yesterday he took me with him to breakfast with Lord Lynedock.

Brussels is a beautiful town; at least the upper part, particularly what is called the Park, which is, however, only a large square. I do not recollect having seen anything so fine in its way. The houses are handsome, though I understand their price to purchasers is very low. The peace will soon make a great difference.

The colonel has a very comfortable billet on the *Marquis Trasigny*, looking on the Park. Having left my servant with the lame horse, I remain at the hotel. A billet was given to me on a marquis in the Park, but the stately style of my reception by a pompous servant showed me that, under present circumstances, I should have been ill at ease.

Yours, &c.,   J. S,

21

Antwerp, July 21st, 1814.

My dear Father,

Returning hither on the 12th, I dined with Captain and Mrs. Old-field. I found a new mess established at our own office, as preferable to the hotel, where it was found expensive and uncomfortable. A sub-scription has been raised for providing all things needful for the kitch-en and the service. Two *francs* a-day is the charge, to which we add our rations. The arrival of the additional company and officers led to this.

14th July.—I found on my return that my baggage had been re-moved into a house almost destitute of furniture, and without stabling. Another billet was sent for; indeed, several, as I found them either unsuitable or occupied. In the latter case it appeared that I had been deceived by the presentation of old billets, the parties having left,

This afternoon was more successful. On calling at a good-looking house, the servant said, on the presentation of the billet, there was an officer already in the house. However, the master being at home, I requested to see him.

On my introduction, after explaining the object of my visit, a billet was produced. He said he could not lodge two officers. I then asked for the officer, but he was not at home; then for his room and bag-gage, but the luggage he had taken with him. The master then showed me his room, and an excellent stable. Seeing I could not be more pleasantly lodged had all the houses of the town been offered to my choice, I said to him, "We shall be very good friends. There will be no late hours. That I should give very little trouble." We have since been very friendly. I have not been so pleasantly lodged since entering the country. My cheerful room looks into a nice garden at the back of the house, free of all the noise of the street. I do not think the lady would like to be deprived of the corresponding room facing the street, to one of the windows of which she has mirrors so placed as to reflect up from the street-door, so that every visitor stands revealed to her view.

I dined this day with Powel, meeting some of his brother officers of the Guards.

19th July.—The Prince of Orange being about to take the command of this army, Lord Lynedock, previous to his retiring, has paid a visit to Antwerp. This morning, about five o'clock, he reviewed the garrison. A few manoeuvres were passed through, after which we were dismissed.

The produce of this country is abundant, and the butter excellent, of a quality rarely met with. The price is from 6*d.* to 8*d.* per pound. Eggs, 4*d*, a dozen. Vegetables and fruit in great abundance.

The colonel came from Brussels on the 21st. I dined with him at the "*Grand Labourer.*" This letter was in hand when word was brought me of his return. Since that time, I have been so engaged with his writing that there was no opportunity of completing it for Thursday's post. This day, the 25th, is the next post.

The colonel left yesterday, intending shortly to return, making Antwerp his headquarters. This may arise partly from the approaching departure of his friend Lord Lynedock, as the Prince of Orange is taking the command.

The colonel has turned out a barouche in very good style, with a pair of good horses.

A few lines from him now reaches me, brought by Lieut.-Colonel Sir C. Felix Smith, of ours. He is brother to the Miss Smith whose interesting *memoir* you have, to whom, though he is similar in point of abilities, he is not so as to the use he makes of them. I have called upon him by the colonel's wish, and go tomorrow morning to Bergen to point out the circumstances of the attack.

With, &c.,   J. S.

Antwerp, 25th July, 1814.

22

Antwerp, 30th July, 1814.

My dear Father,

My last was despatched on the 25th. Early the next morning I rode to Bergen-op-Zoom, to meet Colonels Felix Smith, and Elley, of the dragoons. From the drought and heat of the weather, the greater part of the road was very deep in sand, which made riding heavy work. About nine I reached my destination, the *Cour de Hollande* to breakfast. Two hours later the two colonels arrived. We then proceeded round the fortifications; and, having satisfied them, on the spot, with the history of the attacks, we returned to the hotel to dine. They then resumed their journey to Rotterdam. Somewhat later I rode back to Antwerp.

The weather is so excessively hot that one is obliged to avoid all exposure to it, as much as duty will allow. I am now occupied in drawing a plan of Antwerp. Several of the other officers are similarly engaged in the other fortresses. Those at Antwerp are calculating the quantities of gunpowder, labour, materials, and expense of levelling the fortifications which surround the town.

28th July.—This morning began bathing. Turned the hooded luggage cart into a bathing machine, for which it is not unsuitable, taking me from the house into the water. I go between 4 and 5 in the morning, which, besides not interfering with the duties of the day, seems more beneficial.

5th August,—The weather continues still very hot, but not with that overpowering heat we had for some days. All is quiet. I am expecting the colonel from day to day, but not with any anxiety, as it is not unpleasant at times to feel oneself one's own master.

The fortifications for the destruction of which our men came out, remain untouched. The men not having their regular work, idleness and the cheapness of drink is telling sadly upon them. Some who hitherto promised fair, of whom one hoped better things, are becoming too much like their companions, and are getting involved in the iniquities of the vile parts of this place. Indeed, one feels the state of things around, and a separation from the means of grace deadens the feelings to those better things which only the love of Christ and His Spirit can keep alive in the heart.

6th August—I received yours of the 20th. You allude, my dear Father, to my not taking up the billet on the *Marquis*. It sounds very fine, otherwise, perhaps, it might not have been named. A billet is only for the lodging. Not having, therefore, my own servant with me, I should have had to take my meals out, or to have employed his, at greater expense. So that, considering the shortness and uncertainty of my stay, economy as well as comfort commended the hotel.

Your letter was accompanied by one from the colonel, expressing surprise that one sent from Liege had not been received, dispatched at the request of Lord Lynedock, directing me to go thither and make a sketch of the old citadel and town. Through the negligence of the dragoon the letter was lost.

Immediate preparations were made for leaving my pleasant quarters at Antwerp. Sending my trunk by a conveyance, took my servant on horseback with what was more immediately requisite.

Arriving at Brussels I saw Colonel Smyth, and afterwards went to the hotel.

7th August,—As the sketch at Liege requires expedition he wishes me to go. I shall not have an opportunity of sending a letter from thence, so dispatch this before starting.

From Brussels,   J. S.

23

Liege, 9th August, 1814.

My dear Father,

My last was abruptly concluded on the 7th at Brussels, setting off for this place in the afternoon. My trunk was despatched by the diligence.

Louvain is the first town of any importance on the road. We passed several villages very pleasantly occupying the valleys. The ancient town of Louvain with its fine *Stadt* House and old churches lies in a valley. This is a classical country, having been continually a seat for war since the time of Caesar and his *fortissimi Belgi*. The day had closed before reaching Tirlemont, where the inn afforded a very comfortable lodging for the night. Left Tirlemont early in the morning, halting to breakfast at a village about half way. The peasantry were busily occupied in harvesting the abundant produce of their fields.

This part of the country from Brussels presents a very different appearance from the parts I have hitherto been familiar with, being continuous hill and valley. I had intended to remain quiet during the heat of the day, but as the air freshened proceeded on my journey, reaching Liege at 3 o'clock.

Putting up at the *Aigle Noir* I found none of the welcome with which an arrival at an inn is received. I was not at all satisfied with the accommodation offered, and was about leaving the house. They had taken me for a Prussian officer in my travelling costume, and having found out their mistake, I experienced excessive civility. After arranging my dress and dining, I reported myself to the *commandant*, a Prussian officer, informing him of the object of my visit. I then got a billet, though, having no forage for the horses, remained at the hotel for the night.

I found the master of the house on which I was billeted, in the Place Verte, all civility and politeness. He was a French count, but had left France some years. He said he loved the English, and though he was leaving home on a visit to the country, particular directions would be given that everything required would be left out for my service.

The town of Liege, from the abounding coal, has a dark and dirty appearance, with a quantity of black dust from the road traffic. It appears also to have suffered considerably in the passing to and fro of the armies during the war. The interiors of the houses have lost their neatness and cleanliness.

9th August,—On taking possession of my billet I found the rooms and everything connected with them in the most dirty state, alive with fleas. My very polite host had locked up all that he could lay his hands upon, so that the most common utensils were wanting. However, to make the best of it, everything was taken out that the place might be thoroughly washed and cleaned.

In the meantime, I went to reconnoitre the heights, where are the remains of the citadel of which and the adjoining country I am to make a plan.

Liege is a straggling town on the Meuse. Report says it is to be a frontier town for the Dutch, It is still surrounded by an ancient wall. The prospect from the citadel is beautiful. The features of the country are strongly marked and well wooded. Immediately below appears the town; part on this side of the river, and part on the other. To its churches and buildings, the opposite woody side of the valley formed a background, which, whenever the nature of the ground permitted, was peopled with houses. The winding of the river might be traced a little further, till lost in its woody banks. Behind me was a woody ravine, interspersed with cottages. The whole forms a beautiful picture to which I regret not to be able better to do justice.

While at Liege I was very busily occupied in completing the plan, so had not the opportunity of seeing the surrounding country. Being so near I should much have liked to have rode over to Spa. I dined every day (having no rations) at what is called the *table d'hôte* at the *Pavilion Anglaise*, near my abode.

It is the custom for the masters of most inns to keep a regular table, at which members are admitted according to the respectability of the house. It is very convenient for those who have no families. Everyone is independent. A much better dinner is obtained at a much lower cost than would be otherwise attainable, besides the pleasant society one falls in with. The cost was two *francs*, which includes everything except wine. The dessert in this country forms part of the dinner.

13th August.—Left Liege late in the afternoon. Resting at Tirlemont for the night, dining at Louvain the following day, reached Brussels in the evening. The colonel was out. I learnt that Colonels Pasley and Chapman, of the Engineers, were here with the Duke of Wellington, on the way to Paris; that my plan was in time, as Lord Lynedock had not left. I put up at the *Hotel d'Angleterre*.

15th.—Going up to the colonel's to breakfast, I found that all the party were gone out for the day with the Duke of Wellington; but was greeted with your letter of the 4th. Had you not mentioned that my brothers were making a visit to the Continent expressly for study, I should have hoped to have seen them in this neighbourhood. I do not think I can get any more of those ancient prints. I have only seen them at Middleburg.

The expense of fitting out our mess at Antwerp, amounting to forty *francs* each, will soon be repaid us, as we pay one *franc* per day less, besides having an English dinner, which is no small recommendation. Our wine is about half the price, without the obligation of drinking it. The cost would have been less had more officers been present; but now, from the changes and removals, we have a good sum in hand.

Sir Felix Smith only passed through, making the circuit in his way to England from the Spanish Army.

16th.—Breakfasted at Colonel Smyth's. Colonel Chapman was staying there. Employed during the day drawing a plan of Charleroy for the Duke of Wellington.

Found some difficulty in getting a convenient billet, the town being so full. The marquis being gone into the country, his house is shut up. Finally succeeded and removed from the hotel. Headquarters is in some confusion owing to Lord Lynedock's departure on the morrow.

Dined this day at the Vauxhall in the park. The party consisted of Colonel Graham, Lord L.'s brother, Colonels Chapman and Pasley, the colonel, and self—a very pleasant party.

17th August.—Breakfasted at the colonel's. Colonels C. and P. were with him, who afterwards left Brussels with the duke. Lord Lynedock makes a little circuit to Ostend, where he embarks for England, to which place the colonel purposes to accompany him, returning by Antwerp to Brussels, and taking me up in his way. Rode to Antwerp in the afternoon, passing through Malines. Arrived in time for the mess dinner. Having a letter for Captain Oldfield, drank tea with him and Mrs. Oldfield.

22nd August,—As this is post day, I conclude my letter. The system of billeting is to be done away with as much as possible. Where barracks do not afford the requisite accommodation, lodging money is to be given. This will be a great relief to the inhabitants, as there are some who are not sufficiently careful to avoid giving those on whom they are billeted just cause of offence.

22nd August, from Antwerp,   J. S.

24

Antwerp, 30th August, 1814.

My dear Father,

Having nothing to say of myself, you may like to hear of the people among whom we are. They are now celebrating one of their principal religious festivals, which they call "*Les Carêmes.*" The French did not allow their religions processions and ceremonial outside the churches. That is all changed; now they are sanctioned, and we are directed to respect them.

On Sunday, the 21st, they paraded the streets, bearing about that which they proclaim to be God, and seem to believe in as the only Saviour of the world. The public-houses, which abound much more than in England, and are adapted to the purpose, may be seen filled with the different classes of people met together to spend the day in dancing and frivolity. It is the same in all the villages.

All the lower classes seem to dance here, and by no means inelegantly, so that in a village on the outskirts of a town you may see the houses full of dancers, or the open spaces around, with two or three musicians, giving animation to the scene. The ragged and the dirty foot it in a style not unworthy of accomplished dancers. On Sundays it is carried to greater excess, with roundabouts, and the usual accompaniments of a fair.

I am sorry to add that some of the officers take part in these things, and are drawn into frequenting balls and playhouses on Sundays, to the discredit of our Protestantism. One cannot be surprised that serious evils arise. A court is now sitting on a case of this kind, in which several officers are discreditably concerned.

24th.—Dined with Pringle, and met our chaplain, Mr. James, with whom we had some pleasant converse. He seems in earnest, desiring much to be useful.

Having heard of the gardens of a gentleman not far from Antwerp, I rode there with Pringle. As the gardens here are laid out so differently from ours, I must attempt a sketch of the present one.

Having paid our respects to the owner of the mansion, he gave us in charge to a servant to show us over the grounds. Leaving the house, we walked down a broad walk, garnished on each side with shrubs and flowers, which terminated with a circular sort of rotunda formed of yew, neatly clipped into various figures. In the interior the yew had been so cut as to form niches all around, in which were placed statues. I forgot to mention that the entrance to the house is by a road with ornamental box hedges, cut into all sorts of curious shapes. Following our guide, we came to a lofty Chinese *pagoda* of six or seven stories.

The interior was decorated in a very costly manner, the walls painted in the nicest art. Leaving the *pagoda*, we passed temples and statues; a flock of sheep came in sight, grazing; but on a nearer approach, they proved but images, though not badly done. The shepherd and his dogs were in a sort of cavern. The next object that drew our attention was a neat cottage; the inhabitants, though well sculptured, were not represented under a favourable aspect, but one fears in a state too common, from its also being a favourite subject in their oil paintings.

We now came upon a reverend hermit's cell, with his beads, cat, &c. Passing under various passages we came to what appeared the termination, where the builder, as sensible of the vanity of his labours, had written up what had been frequently on our minds in the garden, "Vanity of vanities, all is vanity." To which was added, "Also the world will end."

We concluded we had seen all; but looking further, we discovered the stoic philosopher, Diogenes, sitting in his tub, holding a scroll. Seeking to approach him more closely, our curiosity was suddenly damped, and we were involved in little jets of water, proceeding from the walls, on the sides, and from the pavement. In making our escape through the archway, that was more treacherous still, as the little fountains opened not only from the sides, and under our feet, but from above also. Coming out, we found our guide had touched a spring, which produced the effect. After seeing further imitations of ruined bridges over the serpentine canals, with which the gardens were ornamented, and other ruins, caverns, fountains, hot-houses, with all sorts of curious plants, we took leave.

There was a feeling of dissatisfaction on the mind after such a sight. When the novelty was over, what remained as the fruit of so much labour? It, however, left a useful lesson on the mind. How little this world can do for us, and how insignificant the various objects which now interest us will shortly appear.

With respect to the garden, we began to be wearied of it before we had well got through the inspection—so much had some of it the appearance of childishness. We were, however, gratified with our visit.

5th Sept.—Yesterday yours of the 15th came to hand, for which and its enclosure I thank you. I had purposed with Pringle a visit to Rotterdam, but his being placed on a court-martial prevented it. We have some occasional deaths now from the fever which prevails in this country about this season. I am, by the blessing of God, quite well. Would that I exercised myself more in that daily dying of which the Apostle speaks.

We are allowed no travelling expenses, except the circumstances are of such a nature as to debar us from using our own horses. Our increased pay is supposed to make up for the extra expenses we are continually liable to in our detached duties.

I am now looking out for the colonel, as he has written to say he shall be here this morning. I hope to send this letter enclosed with the returns to Colonel Handfield.

Colonel Smyth has just now returned. I go to Brussels in a day or two.

J. S., 5th Sept., 1814.

25

Brussels, 10th October.

More than a month, my dearest father, has elapsed without having the pleasure of writing to you. There are, however, many reasons to account for this. Since being settled, I have had an unusual quantity of writing. Praise be to His name from whom we receive all our blessings, I am now somewhat comfortably settled.

However, not to begin at the end, it will be more satisfactory to you to trace my steps from the date of the last.

6th Sept—This and the succeeding days, while Colonel Smyth remained at Antwerp, were much occupied with writing of various kinds. This day dined at Capt. Oldfield's, where I met the colonel, and also Colonel Jones, R.E., who was passing from Holland, going on to Paris. He is the writer of the Spanish sieges.

7th Sept—Rode out with Colonel Jones, who is still lame from his wound. The colonel entertained all the officers at dinner at the *Grand Labourer.* On the 9th he left for Brussels. I dined with Pringle and Anderson, B.A.

10th Sept,—Left Antwerp this morning. Many things made Antwerp a pleasant residence—the society of Pringle and Anderson, who was becoming a follower of the same Saviour, also Mr. James, and a very comfortable billet. On the other hand, one felt a lassitude and headache, which is sometimes the forerunner of the fever which was prevalent. I rested at Malines, visiting its highly-adorned church.

Arriving at Brussels, I found an officer in occupation of my billet. To avoid altercation, I sought another, but found that there were none with stabling, and that the intruder had no right to the rooms allotted me, having no billet. Neither had he any duty at Brussels. On my return, another apartment was given, and my servant was to share the same room with his, which I did not like, especially when his character was ascertained.

24th Sept.—My time has been occupied with different official writings. With the exception of dining with the colonel, or any other engagement, I take my dinner at the *Hotel d'Angleterre*, where they furnish several little dishes of meat, vegetables, and dessert for three *francs*. They are very reasonable in their charges, and so insure a large custom. There are many officers like myself, who have not the advantage of a mess. An order has been issued that all billets shall cease on the 1st October. Being desirous of giving up mine, I occupied myself immediately in hunting up a lodging.

So many English being here, the price of lodgings has much risen. The first day I was unsuccessful, but yesterday succeeded in finding one of comfortable appearance and convenient situation. Though dear for Brussels, I immediately came to an agreement. I am to pay five *louis* per month, something more than 5*l.*, for which I have a sitting, sleeping, and dressing-room, servant's room, and stables, which are confined. What may appear strange, the access to them is by going up stairs. It is accounted for by the house being situated on the slope of a hill. The exterior access is at a higher elevation. I entered into an arrangement with the mistress of the house that she should provide my dinners and the servant's for two *francs* and a half, the rations being given to her. This will be much more comfortable than having to go out every day to dine. Linen of all kinds included in the lodging.

I have moved this day into the lodging with no small satisfaction.

Our office being now established, has brought with it much writing, from the increased number of officers, in transcribing orders, letters, and commencing new books, which still hang heavy on my hands. Before going to the office, I breakfast, as usual, with the colonel.

30th Sept.—Having brought up the office work, I rode out this morning with the colonel to look over some ground which the Prince of Orange thinks would form a good position for an army in advance of Brussels, and which I am to reconnoitre. This employed me the next few days with the putting it on paper. The prince had it on the 6th. The plan was, however, returned, in order to introduce into it a further extent of country connected with the position, which was completed on the 8th, and given to the draughtsmen to copy.

During these days I had a visit from Captain Oldfield and Lieutenant Cole. I expect Pringle here, and reserve for that the exploring the place and neighbourhood.

J. S.
Brussels, 10th Oct, 1814.

26

Brussels, 25th Oct., 1814.

My dear Father,

You wish everything mentioned. Being now a fixture, the usual routine will afford but a barren repetition.

The day after sending my last I rode with a brother officer to the *Palais de Laeken*, built for the residence of the Austrian Emperor. It is less than two miles from the town, upon rising ground.

The interior is finely decorated, but its arrangement does not seem well planned. The building is swallowed up in the lower floor, without any superior room. The hall is certainly beautiful, being the whole height of the structure, and covered by a dome. It is now unoccupied. Buonaparte made it his residence when at Brussels.

English families seem daily on the increase here. Some of the ladies dress in a very whimsical style, and seem to wish to attract upon themselves the stare of the town. They excite the regret of their countrymen and the ridicule of others. Judging by appearances, our visitors are not very select.

The Square, or Park, with the part of the town connected, is beautiful, but the lower town has not what may be called a good street; they are generally narrow and dirty. The latter arises in great measure from the mode of cleansing. Every house deposits dirt and refuse in the middle of the street, which is generally swept into heaps once a-day, in order to be taken away; but often, before this takes place, by the continual traffic of carts, and especially when there is rain, the streets are made very unpleasant, which is particularly felt by walkers, as there are no paved ways for their accommodation.

The lower orders seem to observe none of the decorum usual with us. Something disgusting is continually presenting itself.

The country about Brussels has much beauty, particularly at the season which is now passing away. The woods which line the valleys have a beautiful effect, from the variety of the foliage.

It was pleasant to see the altered appearance of the town last Sunday; such a change from the preceding. Instead of the shops putting on their gayest attire, all were closed. It was no longer the chief market-day of the week. This is owing to a regulation of the sovereign prince. Though too much cannot be attempted at first, we may hope it will not be the only advantage arising from a Protestant ruler. The people seem in general pleased with the Orange Government. The Dutch do not seem to have much sympathy with the Belgians, while these affect to hold them somewhat in contempt. Their religious sentiments being so different, must tend to prevent a hearty union, as well as their dissimilarity of character. The number of our officers is greatly on the increase. One or other is continually paying a visit to head-quarters, so that I am frequently favoured with a guest.

My lodging is in the *Montagne de la Cour*, on the opposite side to the *Hotel d'Angleterre*. The street is rather of steep ascent.

The colonel purposes going to Holland tomorrow.

J. S.

27

Brussels, 21st Dec., 1814.

My dear Father,

I have to acknowledge yours of the 2nd, which, owing to the colonel's absence, was not received so soon as it otherwise would have been. I am sorry to find that you are not well, which probably arose from the anxiety and worry of your suspense about my missing brothers; but, with the cause, is, I hope, now abated. My intercourse with Pringle, since his short visit with Anderson, is now limited to an occasional note.

23rd Dec,—I had intended finishing this letter the other evening, but was interrupted by the post, which gave me other work, which is increased by our added officers.

My last was sent on 22nd Nov., when the colonel was inspecting the fortresses to the South, Mons, and others. I rode over to Louvain, where two of our officers were employed. You may, perhaps, remember my having mentioned C, either in a letter or when at home. Recently his sister (Mrs. Colonel P., not long married) has died. Being much attached, it has greatly affected him and given his mind a deadness to the world. It has pleased God to supply its place with a hungering and thirsting after righteousness.

When I spoke of Him before, though he deeply felt and read the Bible, yet there was the wish, either by constant occupation, or in the society of his brother officers, to silence the uneasiness which otherwise oppressed him. He was one of the officers at Louvain. It was gratifying to hear him now express his love of being alone. As you may suppose, his present circumstances brought us into much closer union.

Being much alone is, I think, in many cases productive of the best effects upon the soul, at least that seems my experience. When much in society the mind acquires a sort of lightness and conformity to the world. When solitary, thoughtfulness is awakened; His presence is looked for, which brings with it peace and joy. The heart is quickened. There is, however, the other side of the picture.

24th Nov,—The colonel returned from the fortresses. Captain Gipps arrived from England; we dined together at *Hotel d'Angleterre.*

Dec. 8th, 1814.—During the past few days there is nothing to note. As we have many officers delayed at Brussels some of them dined with me, except when I dined with the colonel or joined them at the hotel. On the 6th, being the prince's birthday, we had a grand parade and *levée.* I ought to have mentioned that the colonel asked me to dine on the Sunday, and accepted my refusal in a very kind manner.

11th, Sunday,—C. with me.

12th Dec.—C. having finished his reconnoitring at Louvain, has been detained here to finish the drawings. I have had opportunities of enjoying his society and entering upon those topics which relate to the soul and the love of the Saviour. I was pleased to see that he gave a preference to my society. Today I had the pleasure of his dining with me alone. The other officers having got their instructions, left.

13th Dec.—Several proceedings on the French frontier having given rise to some alarm, the colonel left for Tournay and Ostend, with a view to having the frontier fortresses put into a state to resist a *coup-de-main*. Took a ride with C. Captain Oldfield just arrived from Antwerp. Dined with him and C. at the *Hotel de Clarence*.

14th Dec.—C. and Oldfield, with the remaining officers, left for their posts today. Since the increase of our numbers the officers have been divided into brigades, consisting of a captain and three subalterns. A certain district is allotted to each, and they are attached to the divisions of the army.

19th.—Colonel S. returned. I dined with him and got from his budget your letter, and one from Colonel H.

22nd.—I have been gratified with a letter from C. I had given him, when he left Brussels, "The Dairyman's Daughter," which, from its similarity with his sister's case, had affected him in a peculiar manner. He now, indeed, by his conduct shows the power that the religion of Jesus has to change the affections, and to raise the soul to God. Dined with Colonel S.

24th,—I have not been able to detail much more minutely as you wish; there would be an uninteresting sameness, of which one day forms the outline. I rise about 6 o'clock. Go up to breakfast at the colonel's soon after 9. He is not always punctual. Thence I go with any instructions to our office. Have there to see after the reports of our department to the adjutant and quartermaster generals. To circulate any orders to our divisions, as well as to enter the general orders.

When the colonel comes I have to enter his official letters; when there are many I am detained late, but generally speaking, I have time for a ride. When he is absent the omission of this latter duty leaves me more free. The rumour of war seems now subsiding, and congress likely to terminate peaceably. We have had some frost, and I see there is skating.

With much love to all your dear assembled Christmas party,

I am, &c.

28

Brussels, 4th January, 1815.

My dear Father,

I have to thank you for a very kind letter, 19th *ult*, the receipt of which has been long delayed by the contrary weather. White, one of our officers, who is now by my side and dining with me today, is going to England, and he will bring out anything for which I may have occasion. You will have heard of a packet from Ostend being lost. He would most probably have sailed in it, had not his leave of absence been unexpectedly stopped.

My office is now no idle one. Colonel Smyth is moved into another lodging in the Park. He is very friendly.

Colonel Gold, who commands the Artillery, gave a dinner on Christmas-day to the officers here of the Ordnance and Heads of Departments, from which I begged to be excused.

The colonel had intended to give his dinner on New Year's Day; but, as it fell on a Sunday, he, in a very kind manner, said to me he had put it off till the following day.

When one meets with so much kindness around, there seems almost more reason to fear being led into compliances which interfere with the soul's welfare. How much need is there for watchfulness. Impressions so soon wear off that one needs to be on guard with our armour at all the inlets to sin, that no entrance may interfere with the blessedness of a conscience at peace with God in Christ.

The colonel's was a large party of the principal military persons at headquarters. I had the pleasure of sitting next to Sir Alexander Gordon, the duke's *aide-de-camp*.

He with his elder brothers, Charles and Robert, and a younger brother, John, were at Maxwell's when I made my first essay in school life. Lord Haddo had left. As they were at the top and I at the bottom, we came little in contact. My bed was in the large centre room. The Gordons occupied a smaller one leading out from it. Alexander had a fine spirit, very sensitive of what he deemed a wrong, easily led, but not driven. One night, I remember, he came into collision with one of the masters, and it was only after a struggle that the three assistant masters succeeded in binding him to his bed. The elder brothers soon after left. At our Sunday service at the Chapelle Royale, it is pleasant to be near him. The hearty manner in which he joins in the responses is quite refreshing in the general listlessness.

7th January, 1815.—On the 5th was agreeably surprised by a visit from Pringle. He returned this morning to Antwerp. During his stay I have been so much occupied that I have had but little of the pleasure of his society, though I hope that little has tended to show me more of that fulness of blessing which is in our Lord and Saviour, and to lead me from self-dependence to live more by faith on Him, in order to experience the comfort of the promises of the Gospel of peace.

With much love to you all I bring this to a conclusion, as White is starting for England, and will post it in London.

I dine today with the colonel.

John Sperling, 7th Jan.

29

Brussels, 18th January, 1815.

My dear Father,

I have received the parcel today. Many thanks to yourself and the other dear contributors. All is so quiet that there is nothing to interest you. The winter has set in with severity, and I have to bless God that I am not exposed to its blasts. We are hardly sensible of our mercies till we know what it is to be deprived of them. May our hearts be more truly alive to the great mercies with which we are surrounded. May I not neglect the warning voice which calls to me to look diligently lest I fail of the grace of God and be troubled by the springing up of any root of bitterness. May the Lord quicken our hearts in His service that we may enjoy that peace which flows from abounding grace.

I hope shortly to be able to give you a good account of the Testaments and tracts sent out.

27th.—Many letters pass between my friend C. and self. Next week I hope to be able to pay him a visit at Tournay. His letters are very encouraging. May we, my dear Father, and all your circle become more sensible of our own wants and insufficiency, that we may daily increase in the knowledge of the preciousness of Jesus, the sinner's hope.

The colonel is gone to England on duty, and will be absent about a month.

It is reported today that the Congress is broken up. If so, some arrangements will be made as to this country.

My lodgings are about a quarter of a mile from the office. The upper part of Brussels, that is about the Park, is situated upon a flat ridge, which crosses the south of the town. The principal part of it lying in the valley of the Senne, which runs through. The streets are so badly arranged and narrow that the lower town is devoid of beauty. The good houses being generally retired from the street and enclosed, add little to its appearance. There is a very fine view of the town from the upper rampart, and, as there is no smoke like in England, has a good effect. There seems nothing to remark in the churches. The cathedral has large towers.

The Town Hall, in the Market-place, with its beautiful spire, is the most attractive building in Brussels.

The difference between the lower classes of the Catholics and Protestants is made to appear in the comfort and cleanliness of their dwellings, also in their manners.

J. S., 30th Jan.

30

Tournay, 6th Feb., 1815.

My dear Father,

You will perceive by the date of this, that I have been able to leave Brussels for a few days, which I find the more agreeable as my friend C. makes my abode here so pleasant that I shall leave Tournay with regret.

My last was dispatched on the 30th. The following day Captain Thompson arrived from Namur, to take upon himself the command during the colonel's absence.

On the 1st was celebrated the anniversary of the entrance of the Allied troops, by a German parade, with its accompaniments. It seems strange that the Prince of Orange should order all the staff to the Roman Catholic cathedral to sing the *Te Deum*. Concessions to gain popularity here will not be very acceptable to the Dutch generally. Not having witnessed a similar ceremony, I attended with the rest of the staff. It has, however, only tended the more to satisfy the mind that a religion accompanied with such outward show and pageantry, is not the religion of the New Testament.

2nd Feb.—Was engaged with Captain T. in conducting him to the different heads of departments, arranging letters and papers, and preparing for leaving Brussels in the morning.

3rd.—Having hired a cabriolet, the mare was put in the shafts. The attempt was made to arrange the horse as an outrigger, but he proved rebellious, so the servant followed on him.

Passing Hal, Enghien, Ath, stopped at Leuze for the night.

4th.—Setting off early, arrived at C.'s breakfast, with an earnest hope that the blessing of God might attend the visit to both parties. C. had prepared everything in the most comfortable and kind manner for my reception.

We made an attempt to get as far as Fontenoy, to see the celebrated battle-ground. Owing to the unfavourable state of the weather and the roads, we did not accomplish our object.

5th Sunday.—I was glad to see that Captain Smith, who commands our department here, had the church service read to the men.

6th.—The houses of Tournay present a poor and dilapidated appearance. They bespeak the poverty induced by a want of commerce entailed by the war. The fortifications have been partly destroyed. In some parts, however, they are in a tolerable state, or, at least, might soon be rendered so.

This is the time in which the carnival is celebrated. Here, however, I understand from the poverty, which is general among the lower classes, it is little observed. There are, however, a few masks.

7th.—My intention was to have returned to Brussels today, but kindly urged to stay, and the day being wet, my departure is postponed till the morrow. I have a corporal of sappers as a clerk. When a little practised he will be more useful than at present in the office.

J. S

31

Brussels, 11th Feb., 1815.

My last from Tournay concluded on the 7th. Early the following morning I started for Ath, about 19 miles, which I reached to breakfast by 9 o'clock. The town is small, but has a fine appearance from the surrounding country. There are some remains of its former fortifications. I reached Brussels about 5 in the afternoon, the distance being over 50 miles. The country even at this season is not devoid of beauty. Both at Tournay and along the road there is much variety. From the state of the weather and other contributing circumstances, the journey was much pleasanter than anticipated.

Upon my return to Brussels, I found Colonel Smyth was expected. The weather is remarkably mild and pleasant for the season. One is tempted to forget that it is winter.

14th Feb.—I received today a note from the colonel which gave me much pleasure, as you are mentioned. I may conclude you are quite well, for he says you look younger than I do. He infers that we shall be yet a considerable time in this country.

Had not our Lord assured us that men love darkness rather than light, and did we not know that the carnal mind is enmity against God, it would surprise us that the truths of the Gospel could be so perverted as is the case here, and that men's fancies and traditions could be substituted for the clear revelations of the Gospel. They are kept in sad ignorance. For instance, if they want to commit some known transgression, an extra attendance at Mass is given, or some act of penance is performed, whereby they conceive a sufficient atonement is made.

Thus, while the people are educated to use so many outward tokens of remembrance of our Lord, by continually crossing themselves, wearing crosses, and having continually before their eyes images of the crucifixion, and bowing down to them; with all these appearances of devotion and love, which make as if He were the object of their thoughts and affections, yet in all their ways they deny Him in His person and offices. God grant that our love may be something more than an outward form. While others may only have His name on their lips, may we have an abiding consciousness of the presence of the Lord Jesus, His name borne upon our hearts. Then we shall trace marks of His love all around, and praise and thanksgivings will not vent themselves in cold or lifeless forms, and we shall abound in the fruits of righteousness which are to the glory of His name.

22nd.—Pringle has been spending a couple of days with me, with the usual enjoyment of his society.

Give my affectionate congratulations to my brother on his attaining so high a position among the Wranglers, his humility having placed himself in so much humbler a position.

32

Brussels, 8th March, 1815.

My dear Father,

My last was despatched on the 23rd *ult.* I dined with Colonel Gold, R.A., on the 25th. The Congress having erected Belgium into a kingdom, the following day, Sunday, was devoted to military parades and rejoicings. There was an illumination in the evening, with all the attendant bustle. The inhabitants seem much elated on the occasion.

The colonel being absent, there was no occasion for my presence in any of this, but being, perhaps, in the most noisy street I was very sensible of it.

1st March.—C. spent the day with me, arriving from Tournay.

6th March.—The colonel returned to Brussels. I had the pleasure of receiving by him yours of the 16th, enclosed in the small parcel of books, for which I thank you. In your kind solicitude about me, I find you have been speaking to him about my taking more exercise. I hope he does not think that I have been complaining, as he has always treated me with such uniform friendliness. Since his return I have not breakfasted with him, which has its advantages, as the hour was very irregular, and sometimes very late. It sets me at liberty earlier.

It is in the contemplation of what is to be done that so many officers are coming from England. At present those here are occupied as they have been. But now the idea is of fortifying different points on the Belgian frontier as a protection against France, as soon as a plan for the defence of the country shall be settled by a committee of Dutch and English officers. We are then to complete a certain portion. The remainder by the country itself.

This date reminds me of the corresponding one of last year, a day much to be remembered by me. It should lead me to retrace and seek a more lively sensibility to the great mercies by which I have been and am surrounded.

How soon does the mind resume its indifference. Conscious of our own weakness, and that we cannot command our affections, even to those things in which they have most delighted, how does it impress upon us the necessity of cultivating a life of faith and prayer, in humble dependence upon the blessed Spirit of all grace.

The winter seems slipping away before one seems to have entered upon it, and presents a striking contrast to the last. Thus, our time passes on, however unmindful we may be of its progress. We are surrounded with mementoes of our mortality. The heavens and the earth are passing away, but our souls abide for ever. May our gracious Lord write upon our hearts, "One thing is needful," and so bless us that the prophet's language may be ours:—

I will greatly rejoice in the Lord, my soul shall be joyful in my
God: for He hath clothed me with the garments of salvation;
He hath covered me with the robe of righteousness.

With love, &c.,

John Sperling.

33

Brussels, March 15th, 1815.

My dear Father,

Intelligence of Buonaparte's escape from Elba, and landing in France, reached us on the 9th. On the 10th. Major Tylden, R.E., dined with me.

14th March.—White arrived from England. He brought me your welcome letter, and dined.

The report of Buonaparte's rapid and successful progress has put us all on the alert. General alarm is the consequence. For France, according to human probability, there appears no doubt as to the result. Should he continue his progress in this country, our retreat may be as rapid as it was in '94; for though we have several fortresses, yet it is a work of time to provision and put them into a state to resist an attack. In making too large a grasp, we may lose that which otherwise we might have some hopes of retaining.

The inhabitants are much distressed at the probability of becoming again subject to French oppression, from which they have been so recently delivered.

It is different, however, with the soldiers who have served in the French Army. The Belgic officers are reported not to scruple already to drink the French emperor's health in the *cafés*.

The cavalry and forces raised in this country may be only too ready to turn against us. There must be something very prepossessing about Buonaparte to a soldier, for he certainly seems much beloved by them, notwithstanding they are raised by conscription. When he formed his Imperial Guard, he chose young men from the first families, both from hence and other parts of his extended dominions, who, thus torn from their homes, entered upon his service with indignation, yet soon became attached to his person, and proud of their position about their emperor.

Our officers are being distributed in the fortresses, and defensive preparations are being carried out. But, like the Assyrian of old, Buonaparte cannot advance a step further than he is permitted. It would seem that the nations have not yet learnt that the Most High ruleth, and that glory belongeth unto God.

You, I see by the papers, are not without troubles in London.

I think with you about Romaine. I have very much enjoyed his letters; but it is needful to make many allowances, as they were not written to meet the public eye. They seem to describe the genuine impulse of the heart, in which all other things give place to the love of a gracious Redeemer.

I will thank you to look out for a trusty lad to supply the place of my present servant, whose friends write that they wish him now to be put to some trade.

I regret much to part with him; for, though he has his faults, he is exceedingly useful, active, honest, zealous of my interest, and does not scruple to tell the truth to the exposure of his own omissions. From his being so much with the inhabitants, and his natural talent, he speaks Flemish like a native, and makes himself very well understood in French. So intelligent a lad will be a loss at the present time, when we seem likely to be involved in a fresh war. I should take a native, but our officers who have tried them find them such rogues that they can place no dependence upon them. Even the forage we get for our horses they will sell.

16th March,—The accounts from Paris seem more favourable. We are directed by the General Orders to put ourselves in marching order, and to provide the necessary equipments. The colonel has left today, to visit the fortresses.

With, &c.,   John Sperling.

34

Brussels, March 21st.

My dear Father,

The colonel returned on the 19th from the fortresses, having been occupied in directing the different works to be carried out for their defence. Yesterday I dined with him at the *Hotel d'Angleterre.*

Today he is gone to Antwerp. I was about accompanying him, but, as we were starting, a circumstance rendered my remaining at Brussels necessary. In things, however trifling they may appear, the hand of a gracious God may be traced. What encouragement to the exercise of faith, and casting our care upon Him! Why do we disquiet ourselves in vain, while we have before us a more excellent way—"The Lord will provide."

I received the writing-paper today by Colonel Jones, and am writing upon it. By the General Orders, all wheel-carriages are forbidden to those who are under the rank of general. I had just purchased a convenient vehicle, which I must part with. Its place must be supplied with panniers.

23rd March.—As this is post day, and we are under orders to be in continual readiness for a move, I think it better to avail myself of the opportunity to forward this. All the baggage we can dispense with is sent to Ostend.

The inhabitants, are much distressed in looking forward to impending troubles.

May such events as these lead us to live more in the faith of that Divine power by whom all things are ordered with infinite wisdom, both for judgment and mercy. Yesterday I dined with Colonel Gold.

J. S.

35

Brussels, 27th March, 1815.

My dear Father,

The unsettled state in which report places France affords us more time to organise a vigorous defence against this disturber of the public tranquillity, raised up to fulfil the purposes of the Almighty, who, when he shall have performed his part, will come to an end. Amongst many it was anticipated that a peace, which so much contributed to the extension and strengthening of the Papal power and influence, would not be lasting. God's ways are not as our ways. He chooses other plans than suit our carnal views. Little do we deserve peace while He is so much forgotten, and His ways unacknowledged.

The colonel returned yesterday from the Scheldt. We are in daily expectation of the Duke of Wellington to take the command. His name is worth an army. It gives confidence to the soldier. We want now a leader of judgment and decision.

29th March,—I dined yesterday with the colonel. At his recommendation a brigade major has been appointed to our department. He has chosen Captain Oldfield, who served under him in Scotland. We have all now our hands full of work. I have resumed breakfasting with the colonel, as he finds it more convenient for giving orders and directions about office work.

How soon does a worldly spirit find its place in our hearts, and our minds get on worldly cares. One needs to remember, "a little leaven leaveneth the lump."

When once the opening is made, how large does the breach soon become. One foolish thought leads to another, until the heart becomes dead towards God. May God so keep our hearts, that our lips and lives may show forth His praise.

I have bought another horse, called Mouse, from her colour.

Pringle stopped with me on Sunday afternoon, on his way from Antwerp to Tournay, where his brigade is now stationed. He seems always set in the same path, and continues a steadfast walk Zionward. May we have a more realising faith in our blessed Redeemer,

The Guards are moving towards the frontier. The Prussians are collecting in force in the neighbourhood of Namur.

The King of Belgium and Holland made his public entrance into Brussels today, with great splendour and pomp. All the streets which lay in his passage were greatly decorated. The equipages were superb. All Brussels, I may say, were collected to see the procession. In the other parts of the town, the houses all seemed deserted. How would they receive Buonaparte, should he enter as conqueror? The people themselves allow that the soldiers cannot be at all depended on.

31st—We have reports of Buonaparte's advance.

With, &c.,   John Sperling.

36

Brussels, 11th April, 1815.

My dearest Father,

If a longer time than usual has elapsed without putting pen to paper, you will be satisfied with the account of myself. On the day my last was despatched I was dining with the colonel, and before leaving, Sir George Wood, who now commands the Artillery (Lieut.-Colonel Gold being transferred to another post), entered, and informed Colonel S. that he had fallen in with some officers of Engineers at Ghent, who were quite at a loss what to do. The officer to whom the instructions had been given had left the place immediately after his arrival, having lost his head. As there appeared no other alternative, I received my instructions late in the evening, with directions to proceed to Ghent in the early morning.

1st April.—Having made arrangements in case headquarters should move during my absence, was off early. I rode my new purchase, the servant following with the saddle-bags.

Ghent has been allotted for the residence of the French king. What with his court, staff-officers, also English from Paris, and other parts of France, it was difficult to find a place to put one's head into. Ghent is a large and fine town. Though, perhaps, it has not so many houses as Brussels, yet the ground occupied is more extensive. I had not time, however, to think about its buildings and churches.

The object of the proposed works is shortly this. The permanent bridges of the Scheldt are at Tournay, Oudenarde, and Ghent. Works were constructed for defending the two former places. To oblige an enemy to effect his own passage, something was required at Ghent which would at the same time serve as a rallying-point for troops retreating from the frontier.

Finding our officers, we went together over the ground to be taken up, and afterward to the *commandant*, who, entering into the object, accompanied us to the *intendant* of the department, who promised we should have the men required for the works.

2nd April.—We commenced this morning with 250 men. They were set to construct two earthen redoubts, also to reinstate part of the town rampart, which had quite lost its original shape. Besides myself, there were two junior officers of Engineers, and an assistant engineer from the line. Our number of workmen increasing the next two days, they at last amounted to 2,000. You may suppose it no little task, giving directions, and keeping the men to their work, the rather as speaking a different language. Many of them came from a distance, that the labour might be equally distributed among the several divisions of the department. We began work at half-past five in the morning, leaving off at seven in the evening.

I lodged in an inn outside the town, close upon the works, which was very convenient. Officers and others were continually resorting to the king from the French frontiers.

10th April.—The works being now in a forward state. Lieutenant Bolton was left in charge till the arrival of Captain Harris. I returned to Brussels, all the better for the change to constant out-door work from office life. On my return I found the Duke of Wellington had been some days at Brussels. Though he has not yet officially assumed the command, he directs everything. The Prussians are collecting on our left, towards the Meuse.

I have received a chest of Bibles from the Society, and almost fear they will have to go to Antwerp for the present. Dined with the colonel on my return.

12th.—Yours of the 23rd and 3rd have come to hand today. This day's post has also brought the thanks of the master-general for our exertions in putting the fortresses into an efficient state.

13th.—My servant has received a very satisfactory letter from his father, in which he expresses his desire that his son should be settled in a more certain position. At the same time, he would not think of removing him from my service at any time when attended with inconvenience; he therefore leaves it in the hands of God. There I must also leave it, letting the lad follow his own inclinations.

It is in the day's General Orders that the duke has taken the command of the army. The Prince of Orange has one *corps d'armée*, Lord Hill the other. I am going to dine with the colonel.

With, &c.,   John Sperling,

37

Brussels, 25th April, '15.

My dear Father,

From the great increase of the department, we muster now about fifty officers, with a very good field equipment for our department, pontoon train, &c. We seem fairly well off for artillery. Infantry seems our weakest point. Probably the Hanoverians may prove a good substitute. Of course, there is an increase of our office work.

14th.—Dined with our Brigade-Major, Captain Oldfield, and the following day with the colonel. The heads of departments are now somewhat anxious as to their positions, the duke having made so many changes in Spain on taking the command. There is an apprehension of the same now. It is also said that Colonel Burgoyne and the Peninsular Engineer officers who served under the duke in the Spanish sieges expect to occupy Colonel Smyth's position.

The duke took the colonel and some other officers with him early on the 16th to make the tour of the fortresses. They began with Ghent, where I understand the duke expressed himself pleased with the works and their position.

17th.—Rode to Boom with Major Oldfield, where we have constructed a bridge of boats over the Rupel River, which, in case of retreat, would give us a second road to Antwerp. On our return, Oldfield dined with me.

21st.—The colonel returned early in the morning. The duke, I understand, was very well pleased with all he saw, and the exertions of the officers of Engineers at their different stations. Dined with him this and the following day.

25th.—The future action of the Allies does not appear decided. The great preparations making throughout the Continent will hardly end in placing a reliance upon the promises of one who has so clearly shown that they are only binding when it is his interest they should be so.

Paris is the word in most mouths, and many seem almost to fancy themselves there. The army may finally arrive there. With the blessing of God upon the combined efforts of Europe, there is no reason to doubt it. The way is, however, strewed with dangers. All the great roads are defended by fortresses. Much will depend upon the part the people themselves take.

These are critical times. Happy those who are looking beyond Paris! who, while they may fall short of that, will reach a home not made with hands, eternal in the heavens, prepared for them by the all-gracious Redeemer.

J. S.

38

Brussels, 5th May, 1815.

My dear Father,
I had the pleasure of receiving yours of the 24th, yesterday.

May 1st.—Was sent over to the bridge at Boom to report upon its state and strength. It is 290 yards long, formed upon large boats.

2nd.—The colonel said he was going to make a little tour, and asked if I should like to accompany him. At noon we set off in his barouche for Ghent, which was reached in time to visit the works. They are still progressing, and have been considerably extended. Two captains are now stationed there.

The circumference of Ghent is over six miles, besides the citadel, which is now being placed in order, and was thickly studded with workpeople. Great part of the town is protected by inundations; those parts which are not so are being restored. The redoubts which I had commenced were almost completed, and have a beautiful appearance. The duke said there could not be better field works. The ground offered so many advantages that none of the other works come in competition with them.

We dined at Ghent. At 9 in the evening set out for Oudenarde. With the exception of the park, Ghent seems a finer town than Brussels. About 1 in the morning, we reached Oudenarde. At the hotel all had retired to rest, and had to be roused. The house was so full there were no beds to be had. Some mattresses were, however, procured and laid upon the floor. I did not, however, get much rest, and was up very early in the morning. At Oudenarde some excellent works had been constructed, which the goodness of its position demanded.

Having breakfasted at 9, we left for Tournay, visiting by the way a pontoon bridge at Eskanoff, over the Scheldt. It was protected by a *tête du pont*. The country about Oudenarde and the Valley of the Scheldt, with the surrounding lulls, is beautiful.

We reached Tournay about 3 o'clock. Its appearance was very different from that of my former visit. The original fortifications had been in a great measure destroyed by order of the Emperor Joseph. In their decaying state they seemed to remind one of those peaceable times when wars shall be no more; but now they give rise to very different feelings, at beholding all the masses of earth again resume their formidable appearance of regular fortifications.

We went round the works. The colonel then proposed leaving for Brussels, but, at the request of the officers, our departure was postponed till the morning, and we dined at their mess. I took tea with C. and White.

4th May.—At 6 o'clock we were in the carriage. We breakfasted at Ath. I accompanied the colonel round the fortifications, which are here also being repaired.

Having a few minutes at liberty I called upon Pringle, whose station this now is. He showed me an interesting account of the death of Mrs. Colonel Oliver, in a letter from Captain Maitland, now at Antwerp. It must be a great satisfaction to her husband, under such an affliction, to have witnessed such bright hopes, full of immortality and peaceful confidence. We reached Brussels about 6 o'clock. I finished the day dining with the colonel.

9th May.—Things continue much in the same position. From similar motives, probably, both parties abstain from any act of hostility. The French, like ourselves, are using every means to strengthen their frontier. We had a report that Buonaparte, seeing that war is inevitable, had determined to strike a first and decisive blow. Now we hear the contrary, that he will await on the defensive.

I am sending the Bibles and Testaments to the care of Mr. James, at Antwerp, all the British troops being on the frontiers. Under present circumstances the men do not like to encumber themselves with anything extra. All who wish, I believe, have them. At Antwerp they will be useful for the sick or wounded sent to the rear. Pringle said that many to whom Bibles had been issued were asking what they should do with them. With those who know their value this will not be the case, but, with others, who see not in them the Word of life, and the precious companionship they afford, they care not to inconvenience themselves with the burden. I cannot say much for the moral state of our soldiers. From the facilities which present themselves, drunkenness and vice are sadly prevalent.

We have about 22,000 men at work at the different fortresses. From the cheapness of labour, the expense is less than might be imagined. The French are forming a large local militia. Letters pass as usual between the two countries.

J. S.

39

Brussels, 22nd May, 1815.

My dear Father,

13th.—As there was some intention of making use of the favourable ground about Hal as a position of defence against an invading army, I was directed to go thither and make additions to a reconnaissance which I had made some time before.

I left Brussels this afternoon. Previously was obliged to dismiss the servant I had taken on at Ghent, who turned out to be a regular rogue. I took up my quarters at an inn at Hal. Working myself and horses hard, my sketch was finished on the 16th, and I returned to headquarters.

The country is now very beautiful, and rambling over it was very enjoyable.

17th,—My sketch was laid before the duke. Several officers had arrived since my absence. We all dined together at the colonel's. He asked me to go to Antwerp to meet General Dundas, a particular friend of his, who had just arrived there, to show him over Bergen-op-Zoom.

18th.—Left early for Antwerp; breakfasted at Malines. On my arrival called on General Dundas, who proposed going to Bergen the following morning. I found afterwards Captain Maitland, with whom I had the pleasure of spending the afternoon.

19th.—Accompanied the general, after breakfasting with him, in a cabriolet, to Bergen. There is something very pleasing in the appearance of a Dutch town, from the style of architecture and the cleanliness which one does not meet with elsewhere. After making the general acquainted with the circumstances of the attack, we looked over the new work going forward, as the fortifications are undergoing a thorough repair.

20th.—We returned by Fort Lillo, on the river, where we paused, reaching Antwerp in sufficient time to allow of my riding to Brussels, whither I arrived late in the evening.

24th.—Our lodging money ceased. Left those I had so long occupied, and moved into a billet, which, from having more stable accommodation, is preferable.

If one thing tends more than another to promote a closeness of walk with God during the week, it is, perhaps, the spiritual enjoyment of the Christian Sabbath. If the greater part of that day is engaged by this world's employments, how does the mind become engrossed in earthly things, to which, alas, it is too prone to revert of its own accord. The conscience, also, is wounded in thus following in the track of the god of this world. But why am I writing thus, for if our hearts are fixed upon God we shall not want means nor the opportunity of doing His will and keeping His commandments. Greater space may be left for the exercise of faith and trust while we are learning that this is not our home, looking forward to that kingdom wherein dwelleth peace.

29th.—The same pause continues. It may be called an awful pause, while the nations of the earth are collecting together for the great battle.

The duke reviewed this day part of the army at Grammont, consisting principally of cavalry and artillery. General Hill's headquarters are there. The delay has been of service to us. The battering-train and different appendages for sieges have joined us. A great part of the troops from America have also arrived. Brussels is filled with soldiers.

Having now four horses, I have engaged another servant. The baggage is so arranged as to be carried on the horses' backs. Davis has generally to accompany me, while the other man takes charge of the baggage. We are not permitted to use the soldiers for servants, as in the Artillery and Line, having a money allowance instead. If the opportunity offers, send me a small copy of the Psalms, detached from the Bible.

With, &c., John Sperling.

40

Brussel,13th June, 1815.

My dear Father,

With a heart full of vanity, it is always cropping out; and in letters, where one is always speaking of one's self, it becomes a prominent feature. May I not perhaps also say in return that your love to me puts on a magnifying-glass, and that insignificant employments are construed into honourable services. The reconnoitring at Hal was the sketch of a position formerly held for some time by the Duke of Marlborough. Other officers have been similarly employed, so that the duke has made himself acquainted with the best points for meeting an attack. With respect to the works of Ghent, none of the credit belongs to me, as their small beginnings are quite lost in their present importance.

My journal is a blank since my last, being much occupied in the office. There are only items of dining out, or someone with me.

Sir George Hoste has joined us from England, and we are still looking for more officers. Though Headquarters continue at Brussels, the prospect of our moving seems approaching. Many seem to have very sanguine expectations of a speedy termination to the contest.

The change of my quarters was mentioned; and, though my lodgings had some advantages, yet many things render my present abode more agreeable.

Among others, a small garden, which gives an opportunity for pleasant exercise, when, from being in the middle of the town, I should be confined to my room. Also, the family being absent, I am no inconvenience. We begin at the office now much earlier. If there is nothing extra, one gets free at three o'clock; dine about four; take a ride afterwards in the pleasant environs of the town, or before, if engaged by a dinner.

The custom of having dinners cooked out of the house, in this country, is extremely convenient. There is nothing to do but to send to the nearest *traiteur*, or, as we should call it, a cook's shop, and the dinner comes complete, in a set of tin pans.

I am likely to find a friend in Lieutenant Bell, who is appointed to the Adjutancy of the Royal Horse Artillery, attached to Headquarters. He is highly spoken of.

As yet I have seen little of him. In our similar duties, we shall be often thrown together when the army moves.

With, &c., J. S.

41

Brussels, 20th June, 1815.

My dear Father,

I wrote a very hurried line yesterday morning, in pencil, from Waterloo, to go with the dispatches. It seems, however, very doubtful whether it will ever reach you; but, being now returned to Brussels, I take up the pen to give you some account of the important occurrences of the last few days.

What a call for thankfulness to God, who hath crowned our arms with so great a victory, so important in its results. Our loss has been severe, but can bear no comparison to that of our opponents. The victory has been in everything complete.

The judgment and decision of the duke were conspicuous in all his arrangements. One is not surprised at his fame as a general. The soldiers behaved with great intrepidity. The order and regularity with which the battle was carried on seemed almost to ensure success.

Being with the colonel, who accompanied the duke with his staff in the early part of the battle, until, by the various charges, we became scattered, seeking refuge in the Infantry squares, but remaining on the hill, near the artillery, the best opportunity was afforded of seeing the battle.

Sometimes we were enveloped in smoke; shells bursting on all sides, cannon-balls and bullets flying about. Nevertheless, every movement was effected with that order and precision which excited admiration, even in such a terrific scene of desolation, in which were continually multiplying the dead and dying. Horses were galloping about, having lost their riders; others were maimed. Wounded men were limping or creeping to the rear; others, more severely, were being assisted.

During the battle I was sent with a message to Waterloo. If order prevailed in the battlefield, there was the greatest confusion in the rear. Some recruits, Belgian cavalry, I believe, had taken fright, and spread the report that the battle was lost. Brussels was filled with alarm, and the road to it with confusion. I am, however, anticipating my journal, and must resume it.

15th June,—The French crossed the frontier in great force; Buonaparte seeking, with his usual tactics, to overwhelm one adversary first.

The Prussians were driven out of Charleroi, and, after a well-contested field, were obliged to retreat. So sudden was the French attack, that two of our officers, who were stationed there, reconnoitring, were nearly taken.

16th June.—All were in movement to the front. Oldfield and myself were desired to remain at Brussels for orders. The Prince of Orange had been directed to collect his *corps d'armée* in front of Jemappe, where the Brussels road to Charleroi is intersected by the Namur and Nivelles road.

The attack of the French might have been fatal at Quatre Bras, as they were greatly superior both in the number and quality of their troops. The duke, however, reached the scene of action in the afternoon, with reinforcements from Brussels.

The scene changed. In vain the French attempted to force the position, which had the protection of a wood on each flank. On the last attack, about six o'clock, their repulse was decisive.

The Prussians on our left, at Ligny, had sustained the attack of Buonaparte and the greater part of his army, with undaunted resolution, but finally were obliged to retreat to Wavre, with heavy loss of men and artillery.

17th June,—Major Oldfield and myself were ordered to join the colonel this morning. This relieved us from the suspense and anxiety of the preceding day. On reaching the army, we found the retreat had commenced, rendered necessary by the defeat of the Prussians, that our connexion with them might be maintained. It was a beautiful sight, in an open country, to see the cavalry and light troops retiring from hill to hill, while the infantry, thus protected, were withdrawing by the road in good order. The enemy, I believe, had no idea of the position the duke had selected for the battle till the several points were occupied.

Soon after I had reached the army, the duke desired the colonel to have an entrenchment at Brain-la-leud, which was to form a protection on the right of the intended position. There was a company of Sappers at Hal. I was accordingly directed to proceed thither, and order them to march immediately to Brain-la-leud, to make an entrenchment.

My first thought was to shorten the distance by traversing the Forest of Soigny, but I soon saw that, from waterways and cross paths, I should get into difficulty; therefore, hastening to Brussels, I got a fresh horse, for the one I rode had been out all day. Through pouring rain, Hal was reached by five o'clock. Having communicated the colonel's direction to the captain, the company was ordered for marching at six o'clock. I returned to Brussels, and slept there,

18th June.—Left Brussels early in the morning. Joined some officers of artillery on the road. Arriving at Waterloo, found Sir G. Hoste and Oldfield at their billet, breakfasting, whom I joined. The colonel was with the duke, inspecting the position which had been taken up.

The right, a little in advance of Braine-la-leud, which was to have been strengthened with earthworks, had time permitted. The Château d'Hugomont, with its outbuildings situated more in advance in the vale, was occupied, as greatly strengthening the position, which stretched along the ridge towards Ohain, on the left, crossing the high road, on which a farm called La Haye Sainte was also occupied. The duke was making his arrangements for the battle on the admirable spot which had been chosen and reconnoitred some days previously.

When the colonel returned to the village, he was displeased that the duke had not found the company of sappers at Braine-la-leud, which arrived soon after at Waterloo. It appeared that though the distance was about seven miles, from the intricacy of the lanes through the forest, they had missed the way that inclement night, and lost themselves in the forest.

On reaching the scene of battle, the superiority which our position gave us for defence was very manifest. Along the ridge of the hill there was a raised field road, which gave us the advantage of a sort of parapet, and served to screen our infantry from the sight of the French artillery and army drawn up on the opposite hill. Our artillery were arranged in advance upon the summit of the ridge. It was a situation in which they themselves were very much exposed, yet most important as it respected the issue of the battle. All the attacking columns, descending from their own position, and in the ascent to ours, were exposed to its fire.

The infantry were drawn up in two lines of squares, flanking each other, on the slope of the hill, a little retired from the summit, so as to be completely under cover, yet able to act as occasion might require, and capable of resisting any attack of cavalry. Skirmishing parties were in advice and on the flanks, cavalry were also on the flanks, and some in rear of the infantry, to be ready for action as might be required. Some reserves of infantry occupied a rise a little in the rear.

Our position was thus admirable for defence, but not at all adapted for attack, as we should have been subjected to all the disadvantages of our opponents, had any advance been attempted towards them; also, they were much stronger in artillery.

The battle commenced soon after eleven o'clock, by a mutual cannonade, which soon became more general as the parties emerged from each army for attack or defence.

A strong force of French cavalry was sent round to ascertain the position of our infantry, which was concealed from their view. The assaults upon the squares were attended with great loss to the valiant assailants, who were obliged to retire. Our artillerymen had to take refuge in the squares, or lay down under their guns, during the cavalry charges. The artillery, however, remained uninjured. The cavalry suffered in its retreat by the attacks of ours; also, the gunners immediately returned to their post. Hougomont was the scene of animated contest and great loss of life, but we kept possession of it, or rather what remained of it. (*Vide The March to Hougoumont: Lord Saltoun & the First Guards from Sicily, Walcheren and the Peninsular War to Waterloo, 1805-15* by John H. Lewis: Leonaur 2020.)

La Haye Sainte was subject to a similar contest, but there, I believe, we were not so successful.

The French made several desperate efforts to overwhelm us, as the day advanced. It was said that Buonaparte himself led one of the attacks. Notwithstanding all their exertions and valour, they gained no ground.

The Prussians had been expected all the afternoon to make an attack on the right of Buonaparte's position. They had, however, been delayed, and it was not till towards evening that the effect of their approach was made manifest on his flank and rear.

Buonaparte, to overwhelm us by an extraordinary effort, risked everything.

In this confidence an attack was made by the Imperial Guards and Reserve. For some time, the combatants were enveloped in the smoke, and the event of the day was in suspense.

The column, however, was taken in flank and broken. Assailed on all sides, it became a flight. Our infantry and cavalry went in pursuit. Buonaparte's carriage was taken. He himself escaped on horseback. The duke arranged with Blücher that the Prussians, who were comparatively fresh, should follow up the pursuit, to prevent any re-formation of the fugitives.

A quantity of artillery has fallen into our hands, baggage, &c. Such was the confidence of success, that I understand printed proclamations were found in Buonaparte's carriage, dated from "*Mon Palais Imperial de Laken à Bruxelles.*" Such was the presumption which it has pleased God to make foolishness, and only tend to his own destruction.

The artillery, from their exposed position, have suffered severe loss; also, the staff of the army. Pringle, of ours, is wounded in the breast, I hope not dangerously. A bullet through the elbow of my coat, and another on my saddle, have reminded me of my gracious Preserver. May my heart be enlarged to praise His name.

We paused some time on the battlefield. The colonel, thoughtful of some memorial, dismounted, and took up an officer's sword from the slain. It did not occur to me to do the same, nor did I think how soon the spoilers would be over the dead. The night coming on, we returned to Waterloo with light hearts.

On reaching the morning's billet, we found it turned into a hospital, filled with the wounded, and presenting a melancholy sight.

A vacant room was, however, obtained in the village, which accommodated all the Engineer subalterns, about eight in number.

We got some food, and the ready wit of Francis Bond Head, (later the Right Hon. Sir Francis), who was one of those so nearly taken by the French at Charleroi, escaping without his hat, told so effectually upon our host, that he supplied us with wine. After this, most of us wrote a few lines to our friends, to accompany the despatches. For the night, we laid down upon some straw, with our feet to the centre of the room.

J. S., 20th June, 1815.

42

Headquarters Le Cateau,
24th June, 1815

My dear Father,

I wrote on the 20th, giving an account of the battle. The army moved on the following day towards this town, where they came to a pause.

On the 19th I returned with the colonel to Brussels. The road was still in some places almost blocked up by bread waggons, &c. The drivers had in the panic taken away the horses; others had lost wheels. Approaching Brussels, we found its inhabitants thronging the sides of the road, giving expression to their joy at the results of the preceding day, and the more so from the alarm they had been thrown into. I dined with the colonel.

22nd.—The preceding two days I had to arrange for the movement of what office things might be required, and to circulate some orders. Early, this morning I started with Sir Geo. Hoste for headquarters. The colonel had preceded us the day before. The road was still in disorder. Nearing the battlefield, we were sensible of a contagious smell, which increased as we approached the scene of action. Here we were presented with a melancholy sight, for though people had been employed burying the slain, yet the ground was still thickly strewed with dead bodies of horses and men.

Peasants were seeking what they might pick up, and taking the little covering that had been left upon the dead. It was a horrid sight, the distortion of some and the immense enlargement of others.

While it is the lot of some to fall in the field of battle, we are all going the same way. Soon must the spirit cease to animate these perishing frames. May the thought lead us to seek to have part in a glorious resurrection, that this mortal may be swallowed up of life.

From this deplorable scene we rode on to Nivelles, where we breakfasted. Hearing that headquarters had moved in advance, we thought it better to deviate from a road which had been overrun by the two armies. We therefore crossed the country to Braine-le-Conte, and so to Mons. Here we remained very comfortably for the night at the *Hotel Imperial*. We set off on the morning, 23rd, for Bavay, where we had intended to give ourselves and horses some refreshment.

The appearance of Bavay was desolate. It was also crammed with soldiers, so that there was no place to put our heads into; we, therefore, continued our journey to headquarters, which we reached in the afternoon. We had found the latter part of our way, approaching headquarters, lined with troops, who had pitched their tents by the woods. The approach to Le Cateau, with the encampment of the army around, presented a very pretty sight. After a while got into a comfortable billet.

Yesterday afternoon some cavalry and artillery went to Cambray, with the hope that the white flag would be hoisted. The result is not known. Buonaparte is supposed to be at Laon. The French king arrived here this day. My horse, Mouse, turns out much better than anticipated. I bought another on the 16th, making the fourth, but the dealer put me upon an unbroken horse for trial, which bucked and reared till I was brought to the verge of the deep ditch of the town, which had no fence. It was a merciful Providence that I was enabled to slip off at the last moment.

I have to thank you for yours of the 16th, received this morning. I have the pleasure of falling in with Pringle and Cooper. With respect to the wound of Pringle's brother, it was at first supposed the ball had entered the breast, but was afterwards found to have struck against a strap, which it had not penetrated. His recovery was doubtful when I left Brussels. He is now better.

With, &c.,

J. S.

43

Gonesse, July 3rd, 1815.

My dear Father,

My last was sent from Cateau. Here we are making a pause, not without hope that amicable arrangements may be established. It is, however, said that the ruling party in Paris are determined to risk all rather than make the sacrifice demanded by the Allied Powers. The army, it is said, since the departure of Buonaparte, are somewhat inclined to the king.

24th.—Headquarters continued at Cateau, to give time for the coming up of the various equipments. The king made his entry in the afternoon. The inhabitants made us very welcome. Cambray taken by assault in the evening.

25th, Sunday.—Headquarters removed to Joncour. Fell in with Pringle; we rode part of the way together. Found the village very poor, and could afford little accommodation, which, the baggage being in the rear and the servants, we felt the more, as we could get no beds. Citadel of Cambray capitulated.

26th.—Headquarters to Vermand, which had the appearance of having seen better days, though now a poor village. A farmhouse was allotted to us, and we had the same inconveniences to contend with as in the preceding village. One great advantage of the country is the number of barns and outhouses, which almost always afford food and shelter for the horses. Perronne taken by assault.

27th,—Headquarters to Nesle, which, being a small town, afforded comfortable accommodation. Had the pleasure of seeing the arrival of the baggage-waggons, which had been delayed the previous day by thronged roads and the narrow bridge over the Somme. My habiliments had got so torn that it was a great relief to get a change.

28th.—I was dispatched with a message to the officer placed in command of Perronne, and to make observations with respect to the fortifications, and their state. I arrived there about 10 o'clock. The governor kindly insisted on my breakfasting, or rather taking lunch with him and some of his officers. On my showing some surprise at the abundance of his table, he said, that as the French had almost ruined them, they were now living at free quarters. The inhabitants furnished what they required. I afterwards rode round the fortifications. They are so strong that our getting possession arose only from the weakness and hesitation of its defenders. The Dutch now form the garrison.

Having fulfilled my mission, I left for headquarters, which had moved to Orville, whither, passing through Roye, I arrived in the afternoon, after a long and dusty ride. Though the accommodation here was much the same as in other villages, yet, having the baggage, we could make ourselves more comfortable.

29th June,—Headquarters removed to Plessis Longneau, near the river Oise. We had now fallen into the high ready for hitherto our route had been traced across the country, to avoid the fortresses. Every house and village evidenced the track of the Prussians, who had pre-ceded us. Filled with animosity for the great injuries Prussia had suf-fered from Buonaparte's invasions, they vent it upon the inhabitants in their passage.

The villagers, for the most part, had fled into the woods. Their houses had been ransacked, plundered of everything valuable. Of the remainder, some had been burnt or left scattered about the rooms. The drawers searched, and the contents thrown on the floors. Wine and beer let run to waste. This was the state of Plessis, our night's quarters. We had to manage as well we could, but slept in our tents.

30th June.—Headquarters to Louvres. Crossing the bridge of the River Oise, the country is very beautiful. Along roads dusty to excess we reached Louvres. Here we succeeded to Prussian devastation, but a knot of houses was found, over which some officers had, probably, thrown a mantle of protection, where we were comfortably accom-modated.

1st July.—Headquarters moved to Gonesse. Not such comfortable quarters as the ones we had quitted, the place being deserted from fear of the Prussians, whom they dread. The inhabitants, however, gener-ally return when they know that the English occupy their dwellings.

The colonel gratified me this day with the pleasant intelligence he had received of his being appointed an *aide-de-camp* to the Prince Regent, the more flattering as it is the first appointment that has been made from our corps. It gives him the rank of colonel. The leg of one of my horses has been much cut by a chain, which will deprive me of its use for some time.

2nd July, Sunday.—Sent to Major Tylden, who commands the pontoon train at Sarcelles, directing him to select the best places for throwing bridges over the Seine. The bridges had been rendered impassable by the French, excepting at St. Germains, where a great part of the Prussian Army had crossed, to take Paris on the south. St. Denis and Montmartre, to the north, have been strongly entrenched, so that any attack from the north, where we are, would be very destructive.

Returned to Gonesse in the evening. My ride proved a long one, having to visit three places along the Seine—Argenteuil, Besons, Carneres, to enable me to speak as to their eligibility for the bridge. From our proximity to St. Denis, and the uncertainty of things, we are obliged to be continually on the alert.

3rd July.—Argenteuil has been selected for the pontoon bridge, which is in progress. I am quite well, except a little cough from a cold taken from the damp connected with the night in the tent, when I had to sit up writing some orders.

J.S.

44

Neuilly, 7th July, 1815.

My dear Father,

My last was despatched a little before the cessation of hostilities was announced. The rapidity and success of the campaign fills one with wonder. What thankfulness and praise is due to Him who has made our way so prosperous.

5th.—Headquarters moved to Neuilly. Montmartre was occupied by British troops. We passed through St. Denis and its entrenchments, which the French had included in the line of works for the defence of Paris. On my arrival at Neuilly, I was sent to find an officer in the 3rd division; after a tiresome ride, returned late. I am billeted here very pleasantly with the colonel in a house near the bridge, looking on the river. The owner or occupier is a washerman. It is a sort of wholesale business here, and carried on in a very different style from that with us.

7th July,—We were to have entered Paris yesterday, but, owing to its disturbed state, the occupation was deferred until today, when headquarters moved into the capital. As there was some difficulty in the arrangement of the billets, we continued at Neuilly.

8th.—Occupied in arranging the billets of the department. My own is a comfortable one at Recamier's, the banker, Rue Basse des Remparts, all the more appreciated, as, since Waterloo, having been generally all quartered in the same house, it had not been without its inconveniences. The servants had only been able to sleep with their clothes off for one night during the march; indeed, one had not even that advantage.

I was with Pringle this afternoon, who had received an unsatisfactory report of the state of his brother's wound; so much so, that he leaves for Brussels tomorrow. His Christian spirit and tone of mind will not be without its happy influence, though the brothers differ greatly in character.

10th July,—This morning was engaged in getting a suitable place for our office for the department. In the afternoon visited the *Hotel des Invalides,* and walked through the Louvre.

14th July.—Occupied the preceding days either in the office or about some regimental concerns. We have had an inspection of the companies. I continue, as usual; my breakfasts with the colonel, who is lodged at a mansion at some little distance.

By your letter, my dear Father, I see that sorrows abound, and that afflictions are mingled in the cup of this life. In vain do we look for happiness from that which is as perishable as ourselves, and tends to remind us that we must return to our native dust. How many instances of this nature have touched us lately. Wheresoever the eye is turned, it meets with but some fresh memento of our mortality. Oh, that our hearts were more impressive to the lessons continually before us, and that we had more of that wisdom which is life and peace!

While the mind forebodes that which hope trusts may not be realised, the knowledge of the little that separates life from death, time from eternity, constrains us to look to Him in whose hands are all our times.

May His grace soften all our hearts, that they may echo His will. Knowing how needful the dealings of God are to the soul, though grievous to the flesh, may they lead us to realise a life of trust in Him who is "God with us."

Were I not too prone to comment upon the faults of others, while it would be more becoming to be grieving over my own, I might be inclined to say something of that iniquity which seems as a flood to have overwhelmed this capital. All, indeed, seem to be given to self-gratification, to the fulfilling of the lusts of the flesh and the mind. They seem to exemplify the character drawn by the Apostle of the Athenians of old.

With regard to political matters, you will be more correctly informed from other sources.

Outwardly, there is a manifestation of great joy at the return of the king.

J. S.
15th July, 1815.

45

Paris, July 28th, 1815.

My dear Father,

The newspaper of the 22nd brought the intelligence of the death of one who your preceding letter had led me to suppose would not long continue a sojourner here below. When we call to mind the multiplied acts of love and kindness of her who used so frequently to enlarge our circle, who can refrain a tear.

If we have to deplore a loss, how much deeper must be the sorrow of our dear mother. It is not for me to offer consolation to one who, blessed be God, is so much better acquainted with that source from whence all true comfort flows. Our duty seems to be to apply the event to our own hearts, that it may not speak in vain. May we have grace to realise those everlasting truths presented to faith; and as we have received how we ought to walk and please God, we may abound more and more.

I have had the pleasure of receiving two letters, the latter this morning, and am thankful to find my dear mother and sister are better. We have indeed much to be thankful for, and may truly say, God is gracious. Long-suffering mercy has preserved us from the evils which surround us, and are our just desert. How one treads round the same life of vanity; still the same evil heart; and when one would keep the Lord in sight, how soon is a heart departing from the living God to be mourned over, and a vain and trifling spirit. The Lord increase our faith.

29th July,—I have to thank you for the trouble taken for me. With respect to your inquiries after my health, I had, before we entered Paris, a cold, attended with a sore throat. I got a chill from having to sit up late in a tent writing. It confined me for two or three days at Neuilly.

There are all sorts of reports of our movements. I suppose we shall not be long without some change, as the men and officers are for the most under tents which do not keep off the rain.

With many things in Paris, I have been much gratified; with others, only so much as to be able to say one has seen them. Many things are as yet unseen, for, the morning being generally occupied, there is not time to go far.

J. S.
Paris, 31st July.

46

Headquarters, Paris, 3rd August,

My dear Father,

Though I wrote by last mail, again my pen is in hand, seeing it gives you pleasure. The barrenness of my letter must lay at your door.

On the first, I rode over with Bell and Cooper to visit Versailles and its neighbourhood. On our return we went over the Sevres china manufactory so celebrated. Nothing need be said of the magnificence of Versailles, or of the beauties of the great and little Trianon, since you have one with you who can describe them so much better. Suffice it to say, we received as much pleasure and gratification as such scenes are calculated to afford.

The display at the china manufactory was beautiful, and we were much gratified. From the unsettled state of the country, there were few at work.

In such a scene, the thoughts turn to the perishable nature of the various objects. Why so much labour for that which satisfieth not? What shall all these things profit? If, perhaps, half the pains and labour which are taken in decorating a cup, or a plate, were employed in adorning the soul; if half the anxiety which man devotes to things so brittle were turned to the imperishable riches of the world to come, how beautiful, how lovely would that be which now bears all the deformity of sin, and whose end is nigh unto cursing.

We still continue in uncertainty with respect to our quitting Paris. The cavalry have been sent into Normandy. If I thought there was a probability of our being settled here, I should be pressing a visit from my brother, which would afford me a particular gratification.

From the great increase of our army, and its being formed into divisions, the colonel has appointed a commanding Engineer to each, with an adjutant. Cooper is, I am happy to say, among them. His health is not so good as I could wish it. I hope he is not following in the track of his sister.

With much love, &c.,   J. S.

47

Paris, 15th Sept., 1815.

My dearest Father,

An opportunity of sending this to England induces me to take up my pen. I am almost surprised that some straggler has not paid me a visit, which would afford me no little gratification. There is, however, very little inducement except curiosity to bring a person thus far. Few, I believe, but who would be the worse for their visit, except from peculiar circumstances.

Too sad a picture of the unrestrained depravity of the human heart presents itself in the most open manner, without any feeling of shame.

From what one sees and hears, Louis is much disliked. His seat is only upholden by the foreign army.

Everything seems to say there is yet another cup to be drank.

The officers who went to the Russian review have returned very much pleased with the appearance of the men, and excellent order of the equipages. They had not supposed that Russia had attained to the excellency they saw. 130,000 infantry, 28,000 cavalry, 500 field-pieces of artillery, were reviewed. Report gives out that the duke said he will show them something yet; that we are to have another review, in which the manoeuvres of the battle of Salamanca are to be shown.

Paris is full of officers of the different Allied Powers. There is hardly, I suppose, a house but has one or two officers billeted upon it. The mayors make it appear more than this when it is a question of giving additional billets. The clothing of the troops of the different armies is obtained by requisition on the different towns where they are stationed. Before the different armies leave the country, there will not be much that has not been overrun.

A little time since, it is said, the Prussians made a requisition on one of the departments to rather a large amount. The mayor made an appeal to the King of Prussia, who sent him back to the general with an order for a revision of the demand. Offended with his having made a complaint, they had a carriage to the door, and he was immediately conveyed to one of their fortresses. The new mayor was obliged to furnish the requisition a fortnight sooner than the former order. When I may have the pleasure of being with you at Henley it

114

is impossible to say, though I have it in anticipation. A soldier's life is so uncertain that he can promise himself no resting-place; happy if, by grace, he can keep that rest in view with Jesus which abideth for ever.

With love, &c., 　　　　　　　　　　　　　　　　　J. S.

48

Paris, 18th Oct, 1815.

My dear Father,

I lately visited the French school established on the Lancastrian plan, under the superintendence of Monsieur Martin. As yet there are only about 140 boys. The school was established under the last Government of Buonaparte. As they use the Testament, and none of the Roman Catholic books, it is doubtful how they will be tolerated by the present Government.

From the very prevalent system of profaning the Sabbath, there seems at present no probability of their being able to effect anything like a Sunday-school, even among those who profess themselves Protestants.

Speaking of schools, ours established in the companies of sappers are very satisfactory. When other occupations do not prevent, four hours each day are devoted to reading, writing, arithmetic. The men are thus preserved from some of the evil consequences attendant upon idleness. As the school-rooms are formed of their own rustic construction, from materials at hand in their different cantonments, it is the more interesting. How much so, when we consider God can enlighten the most ignorant, and bless His Word read, to the conversion of their souls.

Since my last the troops are gone into cantonments in the neighbourhood of Paris, to be sheltered from the weather. They talk of our moving from hence in about a month, when the fortresses will be delivered over to us.

I shall soon have completed another year, marked with mercies like the preceding. How greatly do I need God's grace to abound towards me, that my life may exhibit a sense of His infinite compassion and love.

With my different occupations my time is taken up. I have no occasion to say, What shall I do? each leisure moment finding many claimants. Much, however, is unprofitably spent.

The more we realise Him who is unseen, and live in the practical exercise of faith, so much the more shall we know of Him; and if to know Him is life eternal, every step leads onward to that knowledge. How superior is this to a life which has no definite object.

We hear men, who are looked upon as sensible, complain that they want something to exercise the mind, where the result has an interest, and awakens the energies.

The salvation of the soul seems the very thing to awaken all the energies and feelings of the man.

Alas, that men should be drawn to the gambling-table for that excitement, which degrades the mind, and can only afford a bitter source for future regrets!

While the mind of man is so constructed as to need some special interest, may we be careful that the pre-eminence is well established upon Him who is revealed as the beginning and the end, the fulness of Him who filleth all in all. With our Lord Jesus are called into exercise the most ennobling faculties of the mind. With Him we find pardon and peace, through His own precious blood shed upon the cross. With Him it is, Only believe, and thou shalt see the glory of God.

"Could not this man, which opened the eyes of the blind, have caused that even this man should not have died?" Yes, more than this, for He could raise him when dead.

May we have grace to trust in Him, that our dead affections may be quickened into spiritual life, that our life may be hid with Christ in God.

We may, indeed, be termed unsocial; though, by grace, I hope to all we shall show that love actuates our conduct, though we may not conform to what the judgment condemns.

Arrangements are making for our removal, and it is thought a month will terminate our residence in Paris.

With love,   John Sperling.

49

Paris, 11th Dec, 1815.

My dear Father,

More than usual occupation has led me to defer writing. The arrangements for the army are now out. Many regiments are going to England, and nearly half of our officers.

We expect to leave Paris towards the end of the month, to occupy the different fortresses named in the treaty. Pringle is among the number of those who are going home. I trust others may be raised up to supply his place, and am not without hope that here one and there one are rising up to follow in his steps.

I have to be present at a very melancholy scene early tomorrow morning. One of our men, irritated by blows, and, I believe, undeserved provocation, in his passion thrust his sword through the body of a serjeant. In a civil court it would have been manslaughter, but, as a military case, he is sentenced to be hung.

Owing to some difficulty in the case, he has been in a state of uncertainty as to his end for some time.

The sentence at length is decided. While we must all join to detest the crime, for which life is justly forfeited to human laws, yet, before that God who judgeth the heart, and who seeth not as man seeth, who requires much from those to whom He hath given much, I cannot refrain from hoping he may find mercy, through that atonement in which he professes to trust.

He is a quiet, and apparently sensible man. His sentence was made known this morning. He shows the same calmness and resignation to the will of God, with the awful opening to eternity so near, as he did previously.

While we are placed in those situations where education and example alone would put a restraint upon violent action, it should make us thoughtful in the daily temper and little actions of life; for, before God, we may be equally culpable with those who have lifted up unrestrained hands.

Morality may regulate the outward man, but we must go higher to regulate the heart. We must have the mind of Christ.

We are beginning to make our preparations for moving. As soon as the roads are cleared of those who are going, either to the Netherlands or to England, we are to take our turn. I think I mentioned that Cambray was to be our future headquarters. The British are only to occupy four fortresses. The fortresses in the Netherlands will be delivered over to their own monarch. The army is becoming somewhat scattered, only headquarters and part of the first division remaining in Paris and the neighbourhood.

J. S.

50

Paris, Jan. 5th, 1816.

My dear Father,

I take an early opportunity of acknowledging the receipt of your very welcome letter of the 20th *ult.*

Commissioners have been appointed from our army to receive over the different fortresses; but, from some difficulties, our troops have not yet entered, and our stay at Paris is prolonged. The greater part of the army is cantoned between Paris and the fortresses. In the Netherlands, we are delivering over everything to the Dutch.

Not often seeing my dear mother's handwriting, perhaps on that account the few sweet lines she wrote were the more interesting, and increased the gratification and pleasure I felt in reading them. Perhaps if my dear mother knew half what I felt in perusing what she indited, I might hear again.

Some alterations are spoken of in church matters. However, it will not do to go too fast, though something of the sort is wanted. From being too rich, the clergy are now become too poor. The stipend of a bishop is something above four hundred pounds a year; first-class clergy, sixty pounds; second, fifty; third, forty pounds a year in our money, which is inadequate to a decent maintenance. They have a house and garden in addition, and may probably make some levies from their congregations. The consequence is, however, the clergy are not much respected, being generally taken from the lower classes of the people. My next will be from Cambray (d.v.).

J. S.

51

Cambray, 8th Feb., 1816.

My dear Father,

We have at last moved to Cambray, which has delayed my writing to you. I took leave of Paris on the 27th, and arrived here on the 2nd. Since my arrival all has been bustle and confusion on account of the difficulty of finding accommodation for all our people. My time has been completely taken up or wasted. I have got into a quarter which will bear no comparison with my pleasant abode at the Recamiers, at Paris. In taking leave of Madame Recamier, she thanked me that my abode with them had been no inconvenience. Latterly, indeed, she might have parted with me, but she preferred an allowance from Government. She spoke of my "gentil" lad. I made her a present of some English dinner cutlery.

Paris was left without regret, though from the many happy moments I had passed in my abode there, and the uniform kindness experienced from the inhabitants, will always awaken pleasing recollections of the many mercies received during my stay.

I find, by a kind letter from Colonel Handfield, that you have left Brighton, and are now settled at Park-place, which I hope you will all find as comfortable and pleasant as anticipated.

I sometimes could look with regret on the quiet, comparatively speaking, inhabitants of England, while so unsettled myself, were I not reminded that we are at best but strangers and sojourners on this earth, and that the fewer inducements we have to love the things of the world, the more shall we be inclined to seek the unchangeable riches of the future. All situations are, perhaps, tempered with their advantages and disadvantages. It is a beautiful admonition of the Apostle, "Be careful for nothing, but in everything, by prayer and supplication, with thanksgiving, let your requests be made known unto God." In the fulfilment of this may we look for the promised peace.

Our march here from Paris was rendered pleasant by the frost. Most of the great people posted, which was, however, an advantage for those who did not, as we were so much better accommodated. It was enjoyable riding through the country. Colonel Smyth talks of returning to Paris to join the duke, who is about to make the tour of the different places occupied by the Allied Army; after that he talks of going to England for some time.

J. S.

52

Cambray, 1st March, 1816.

My dear Father,

Though my quarter is not exactly what I could wish, yet there are many reasons for preferring Cambray to Paris. Perhaps not the least is the greater respect shown to the exterior of religion. Anything is better than an utter disregard, and those Deistical principles which lead away and blind those on whom the truth has made no deep impression; who, becoming blind to the fixture, seek only self-gratification. It is better, however, to look at home, and see how God is forgotten, and not made the end of every duty. It is a precious thought to keep before us, a "life hid with Christ in God."

Many thanks to you and my dear mother for the letter now received. Colonel Smyth is returned from Paris, and goes very shortly to England.

Through the French Testaments, I have become acquainted with the Bishop of Cambray. The owner of the house with whom I am lodged is an architect, or, rather, a builder, and the principal one in the town. Being employed in the reconstruction of the College of the Diocese, and other church buildings, he is constantly with the bishop.

One of the priests, in calling, had seen my French Testaments. After some demur, whether it was right or wrong, he asked for one. *Monseigneur* heard of it, and sent for one through my host. In sending it, I expressed a wish to see him, to which he returned a very obliging message.

I called, in consequence, with my friend the builder, and had a very interesting conference with him for about three hours. The bishop is rather beyond the middle age. His manner is pleasing and kind.

Our conversation turned very much upon the differences between Catholics and Protestants, with which he intermixed many profitable and useful remarks.

He divested the Roman Catholic religion of many things which are commonly attributed to it. He is, however, one of Buonaparte's bishops, and probably himself much more liberal than the majority. He maintained other positions, which we can only attribute to their traditions, and which they can only vindicate as being handed down by an infallible Church, no foundation for them being found in Scripture.

He lamented greatly the ignorance which prevailed among the different classes, and the unwillingness that existed to devote any part of their time to religion, or even to spare their children to be taught the first rudiments of the knowledge of their Creator.

He said it was not the scarcity of Bibles, but the unwillingness of the people, who would not read them when put in their way. I question whether they ever had the simple French Bible put in their way.

Those I have been instrumental in giving away appear to be highly prized, and I am willing to believe are diligently read.

The bishop did not seem to object to my distribution of the Testaments, but said he looked upon it in the same way as we should on a Roman Catholic translation circulated in England, for though, generally speaking, the sense is the same, yet there are some slight differences which favour the Protestant system.

He published an exhortation at the beginning of Lent, which, though a little of it may appear to us ridiculous, yet he reproves very sharply, telling the people plainly of their state, and comparing them to the Jews of old. Part of the judgments poured out on that unhappy nation had already afflicted their country, and he calls upon them very earnestly to repent, lest the rest should follow.

It would not, perhaps, be difficult to trace the source of the gross darkness which abounds, making the people ignorant even of the first principles of Christianity.

We should, perhaps, say that they were kept in darkness, and though some more enlightened minds may discern through their ceremonial that Jesus Christ is the sum and substance of all, yet of how many does their apprehension not reach beyond the block or stone before which they fall down to worship.

I think it was mentioned that my abode did not exactly suit, though the pleasant terms I am on with the people of the house would almost render any place agreeable.

My host has shown me a cottage which he has in a pretty garden in the town, which he thought I might prefer, while it would restore to his use the principal room of his house. The little cottage will be very pleasant, especially in summer. It has two small rooms on the ground floor, two attics over. It is covered with clematis. He is now adding a kitchen. Stabling will be built. I am to give a trifle for the produce of the garden. It is full of roses, and very productive apple and pear trees of a superior sort, cut and trained in a way quite different to ours.

It will be some little time before it will be ready for occupation. Additional furniture also has to be supplied.

J. S.

53

Cambray, 5th June, 1816.

My dear Father,

It seems strange that while my thoughts are so often with you all at Park-place, so long a period should have passed without my writing to you. I hardly know what has prevented it, except the little passing events of the day, which have not anything of interest.

The bishop paid me a visit a few days since, in what he calls my little hermitage. Captain Bell was dining with me previous to his going to England. As *monseigneur* was accompanied by his vicar, we were thrown a little into confusion. I called upon him this afternoon, and he made me accept a case of mathematical instruments. The bishop, for relaxation, occupies himself in mechanics and optics. He is making a telescope, and wanted some glass not to be had in France. I was enabled to get that and some other little things from England. He also takes great interest in his garden, and has a magnificent collection of tulips. He has a variety of plans for multiplying the sorts.

The duke gave a grand ball and entertainment a little time back.

The invitations were very general. I mention it because there is only the party wall between my garden and his at the back of his house, so that the harmony was very audible.

We have formed a book society among the officers, which is a good thing. So much entrance money and so much subscription is paid. A committee purchase approved books, which, when done with, are sold. Various reading is thus supplied at little cost. I have also the use of the bishop's library.

The sermons of our chaplain, Mr. Briscall, are generally to the purpose, adapted to his hearers. He seems much in earnest, can reprove, and that sharply; too much occasion is there for it. Though one thing is wanting, yet last Sunday, particularly, his words seemed calculated to affect the hearts of his hearers, if not indeed hearts of stone. Hardly, however, out of the church, when balls and horses occupied the tongues of those whose hearts, it is to be feared, had been more with them than the preacher during the service of God. The duke has attended the church the last two Sundays. One disadvantage of his coming is, that the service is very much curtailed—why or wherefore I know not.

Yesterday Colonel Sir Colin Campbell took me with him on horseback to the Convent de St. Martin, at Castelet, about ten miles from hence. The duke thinks of making it his summer residence, and wishes therefore to know the accommodation it affords. It is part of the church property that was sold at the Revolution. It is an immense house, and well fitted up, with large gardens.

My work was to make a rough plan of the house. Castelet is remarkable from the Scheldt haying its source there; also, for a canal pierced through a hill three miles long, and arched over.

Upon our return, I laid down the plan on paper—a little hurried, indeed, as the duke was leaving for Paris in the morning—and took it over to his house. The duke had a party to dinner that day. I had an invitation to the dinner, through Sir Colin Campbell.

I find my little domain a great comfort. It is surrounded by a high wall, which gives it entire privacy. It enables me to take pleasant exercise, when otherwise I should be confined to my room. For the quiet repose of the Sunday, it is delightful. There is also an additional reason to be thankful at having quitted my former abode, as a theatre is being built opposite to it. I also see they are engaged in laying out a racecourse.

I am a frequent guest at the colonel's, who has completed his house arrangements. The office business is much diminished. My Sunday wholly disengaged.

J. S.

Not to weary my readers now that the letters are brought into comparative still life, it is quite time that they should be brought to a conclusion.

Perhaps there may be those who may deem it an impertinence that they are intruded upon a busy world.

In taking leave of those who have accompanied me for three years of my more active career, my prayer is that God may mercifully guide them and myself in the path of the just, which shineth more and more until the perfect day.

Château de Gomont.

Front Entrance

Back Entrance

Interior with remains of Chapel

8 Oct. 1834.

VIEWS OF HOUGOUMONT IN 1834

A History of the Royal Engineers During the Period Covered by Sperling's Narrative

By Whitworth Porter

The disasters encountered by the French Army in the retreat from Moscow, and the consequent necessity to concentrate as far as possible all the outlying Imperial forces to create the nucleus of a fresh army, led to the reduction of the French garrisons in Holland. The Dutch were not slow to take advantage of the opportunity thus afforded them to revolt against the alien Government under which they had so long been writhing, and to recover their national independence. In this they were only partially successful. The open country fell into their hands, and the French were driven into the various fortresses. They were, however, utterly unprovided with any organised force, and so long as there remained spread over their land a number of fortified posts of greater or less importance, garrisoned by the enemy, it was impossible for them to maintain their newly-acquired liberty.

To support their efforts, and to endeavour to recover their fortresses, an expedition was sent from England in the winter of 1813 to act in conjunction with a Prussian corps under General Bülow. The British force was placed under the command of Sir Thomas Graham (afterwards Lord Lynedoch), and under him were Major-Generals Cooke, Mackenzie, and Skerret. The Engineers who were attached to the troops were Lieutenant-Colonel Carmichael Smyth, C.R.E., Captains Sir George Hoste and Thompson (the latter of whom commanded the Fourth Company of the Second Battalion of Royal Sappers and Miners, having Sub-Lieutenant Adamson under him), Lieutenants Abbey (Adjutant and Quartermaster), Sperling, Hayter, White, Cooper, and Eyre. (Lieutenant John Sperling wrote a very detailed journal of all the operations in the expedition in which he was concerned; from this work much of what follows has been extracted.)

The force arrived off Helvoetsluys on December 15th, 1813, and was landed on the 18th at Williamstadt. The Engineers were rapidly pushed to the front by Steinbergen to Tholen.

Sperling's journal says:—

Our party consisted of Captain Thompson, Abbey, Cooper, and self. Tholen, where Sir Thomas Graham and Colonel Smyth were, was our destination. The resting-place for the night was Steinbergen, about ten miles distant. Rain had set in; the road which lay along the dyke was in a wretched state from the previous traffic; the horses frequently could scarcely walk from the depth of mud. We had some difficulty in tracking our way, from our ignorance of the country, and the peculiar arrangement of the roads following the dykes. Night overtaking us added to our perplexities. We were delighted at length to find ourselves in a town.

December 19th. Being obliged to resume our route, we prepared our horses and set off for Tholen. We passed near Bergen-op-Zoom, still occupied by the French I fell in with Colonel Smyth, who had been admitted blindfolded into Bergen-op-Zoom with a flag of truce, to induce the *commandant* to surrender, who declined, stating he was fully prepared for an attack. He (Smyth) was with Sir Thomas Graham.

The first Engineer operation was the construction of a bridge of boats at Zandwarbreiten.

December 31st. By the exertions of Abbey, our adjutant, the previous day, enough boats had arrived during the night for stretching across the river. By break of day, we were at work, only ceasing with the night. There were five boats and the wherry, which obliged us to place them further apart than should have been done could more have been obtained. The other materials were chiefly procured from Oudenbosch. Considering the preparation of the materials, credit was due to the men for the zeal with which they worked. In the course of the afternoon Sir Thomas Graham passed over first, accompanied by the Colonel (Smyth), who gave me an expression of satisfaction. Afterwards cavalry and waggons followed. (This bridge is referred to in

Pasley's *Elementary Fortification*.)

The next incident of importance was the attempt to destroy the French fleet which had taken shelter within the basin of Antwerp. It was thought that batteries could be constructed, and a sufficient amount of fire brought to bear on the fleet to effect its destruction without the necessity of capturing the fortress, an operation quite out of the power of the limited force then available. An advance was made and the place invested by the British and Prussian Corps. Batteries were then thrown up.

Sperling's *Journal*:—

February 2nd. Having reported myself to Colonel Smyth, he gave me directions for the construction of a mortar battery, and to take the Sappers under my charge with me. I understood thit Sir G. Hoste, Capt. Thompson and Cooper had somewhat similar employments elsewhere. On arriving at the place for my battery, I found that spot had been selected because the garrison had commenced a defensive work, which would save us much labour. Ferdinand's Dyke extends from the river nearly to Merxem (a village in the suburbs of Antwerp), affording complete cover from the artillery on the side away from the town. To remedy this, they were constructing the work which in part now served us for a parapet, and brought us much nearer to the docks than any of the other batteries in progress.

There were altogether five batteries thrown up—one for six 7½-inch mortars (the one referred to above), a second for four 10-inch mortars and two 8-inch howitzers, a third for three 12-inch mortars, a fourth for four 11-inch mortars and two 24-pounder guns, and a fifth for three 24-pounder guns. Most of this ordnance was French and Dutch, picked up in the country, and very inferior.

Sperling's *Journal*,—

Soon after three o'clock (on the 3rd) the batteries opened at the same time on the shipping. The colonel sent Hayter to assist Capt. Thompson, who was occupied in finishing the battery for the 24-pounders, which was more exposed than the others, the French having constructed a battery in advance of the fortifications, which fired right upon it. I accompanied him. The battery was in a garden near the house, and there were many trees around. We had not been long here when the scene became not

a little appalling, the whiz of the shells carrying death and desolation, the crash upon the houses, the branches of the trees split
and falling about. Considering our position very few suffered.

The bombardment was kept up with great spirit on February 3rd,
4th, and 5th, but on the 6th General Bülow withdrew the Prussian
Corps, which was called away to Brussels. The British force being by
itself insufficient to support the attack, it was abandoned. Even had
this not been done, it is very doubtful whether the object aimed at,
viz., the destruction of the fleet, would have been attained, owing to
the insufficiency of the artillery power.

The vessels, although repeatedly struck, were never seriously injured, nor was it possible to set them on fire, as the crews were able
to extinguish all outbreaks before they could attain strength. Colonel
Smyth, in his report on the operation, remarked that in order to destroy shipping by shells it was necessary that such a rapid and extensive
fire should be kept up as to prevent the possibility of putting out the
flames.

We now come to the most daring operation of the campaign, one
which was brilliantly conceived and skilfully executed, and yet which
failed in an unaccountable maimer on the very eve of success. This
was the attack on Bergen-op-Zoom. Sir Thomas Graham having obtained ample information from repeated and close reconnaissances
of the fortress, considered that in spite of its great strength the place
could be surprised by a *coup-de-main*.

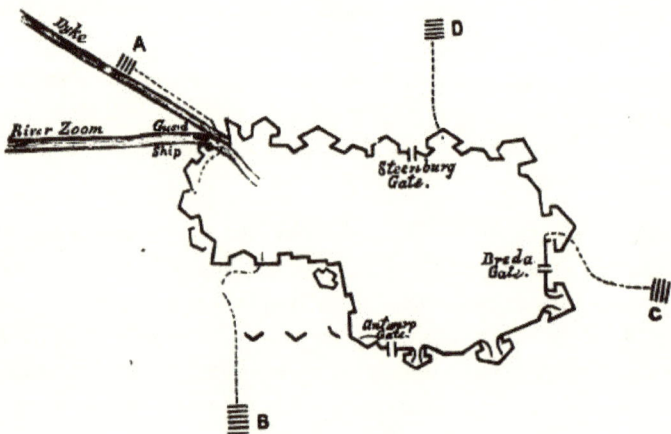

THE ASSAULT ON BERGEN-OP-ZOOM.

It was ascertained that where the River Zoom passed through the *enceinte*, there was at low tide only two feet of water, and that at this point an entrance was practicable; further, that the escarps generally were low, many of the fronts only demi-revetted, and three bastions not revetted at all.

At this time the water in the wet ditches was all frozen, and it had been found that the ice had only been broken by a narrow out in the centre, which could be very easily passed upon planks. The frost, moreover, had rendered it impossible for the garrison to avail themselves of their water defences by opening the sluices. Taking all these points into consideration, and knowing that the very audacity of the project would render it unlikely to be guarded against, Sir Thomas Graham, in conjunction with Colonel Smyth, drew up the following scheme for the assault:—

A column of 1,100 men (A) was to enter by the bed of the river, overpower the guard, and on reaching the rampart turn to its right to assist column B of 1,000 men, which was to penetrate by escalade, the ditch in its front being dry, and the bastion only demi-re vetted. A third column (C) of 1,200 men was also to enter (at the spot indicated in the sketch) by escalade, the bastion selected for the purpose being demi-revetted and having no outworks. At this point a large pond had been formed by shutting the sluice through which the River Zoom entered the town, and in consequence of this inundation no outworks had been constructed on the front.

The pond being at this time frozen over, access could be obtained to the crest of the glacis without difficulty. A fourth column (D) of 650 men was to make a false attack on the opposite side of the fortress to that by which column B was to enter. This, it was anticipated, would much distract the defence. The following account of what took place is extracted from Sperling's *Journal*, he having been appointed to guide column A:—

Between six and seven o'clock (8th March, 1814) I received a message to come to Major-General Skerret's, where his staff and a party of officers, among whom was Sir G. Hoste, R.E, were finishing dinner. He (Sir G. Hoste) had been sent over from headquarters with instructions for an attack that night upon the fortress of Bergen-op-Zoom, which he had communicated to the general. He now entered more into detail with me as to my part. The object was to take the garrison by surprise; ten o'clock was named for the hour of the assault, which had been fixed in reference to the attack by the river, as it was low water at that time; otherwise, a later hour would have been in every respect preferable.

He gave me a note which stated that I was to put myself under the orders of Colonel Carleton, who commanded that portion of the 44th Regiment with the army, to lead the storming party entering by the river into the town. A tracing was shown me of the fortifications where our attack was to be made. First there was the dyke to be crossed close under a battery which commanded its whole length. Then the descent into the river, the position of the guard-vessel in the middle of the river, with spiked harrows fixed at the bottom of the river on each side of the vessel and in front of it. The vessel itself and the entrance by the river were protected by two light pieces of artillery placed at the bend of the river into the town.

These obstacles being overcome, we were to mount the right bank of the river a little beyond the guard-vessel, where stood the guard-house. Before entering the body of the place there still remained some palisades to be passed, and a bridge over a curve of the river communicating with the outworks. . . . . . . At the appointed hour we were paraded to the number of 1,100 men, under the command of Major-General Skerret and Brigadier-General Gore. (Sperling's published *journal* says 11,000 men, but this is a palpable clerical error for 1,100, although, curiously enough, it is repeated a second time.)

A selection was then made for the advanced party or forlorn hope, who were placed under Carleton. My place was with this party with seventeen sappers, furnished with various tools and implements for clearing away palisades or other impediments to our progress. We walked in front, taking the lead with the guide, who was given in special charge to two men never to lose sight of him. . . . . . . At last, the dyke was reached, and we commenced filing along it to the fortifications, having in our face the battery, which swept the whole length of the dyke on both sides. . . . . . . "It was barely ten when the sound of distant firing reached us. The alarm was thus given. There was no time to be lost. We scrambled up as well as we could the slippery sides of the dyke. The battery opened its fire, accompanied with one of small arms. Our safety consisted in rushing forward.

Royal Engineers, 1813

As we jumped into the river, the guard, panic struck and igno-rant of the extent of the danger, hurried out of the vessel, and we, getting through the spikes and water, followed its defend-ers up the river. I was a little in advance of the colonel, who turning suddenly to the right, got up its bank, crying out, 'I am in first.' We hastened to the guard-house, which was almost deserted, the men being occupied upon the ramparts firing at our people who were crossing the dyke. They made little de-fence and gave up their arms, bewildered by the suddenness and boldness of the attack. The officer of the guard surrendered his sword to me.

Having disarmed the guard, we took them with us. Our party consisted only of the advance. Those following were checked, and left the advance unsupported on account of the fire from the other side of the river. (The fact was, that the next portion of the column turned by mistake to the left, and on the rising of the tide became cut off from their comrades.) We now pro-ceeded to the palisades, which presented no obstacle, the gate having been left open. The bridge over the river, which formed the communication between the town and outworks, was not drawn up, thus affording a free passage.

Here, according to our instructions, we took to the right hand along the ramparts. General Gore agreed with Carleton that it was better not to pause for the rest of the column, but to advance rapidly to prevent the rallying of the different guards, and with the prospect of meeting General Cooke's column (B). In our progress along the rampart, at first, we only fell in with the sentries, and then larger parties. They were all disarmed, the muskets being thrown over the rampart into the ditch, and the prisoners following in the rear.

We came to a halt about the fourth bastion, disappointed as to meeting General Cooke's column, of the place of whose entry by some oversight we had not been informed, though we were now near the very spot, but they were very late. Our bugle was sounded, but in vain we listened for any response. I do not think our party exceeded one hundred and fifty, probably under. Our prisoners were, however, more numerous, which in the dusk gave some importance to our party. Again, we resumed our progress along the ramparts to prevent the assemblage of our opponents. It was found it did not answer to stand to fire, as our adversaries did the same, but when we ran upon them, they either surrendered or made their escape down the slopes.

Our men, however, could not be kept from firing, which in the darkness was dangerous to ourselves. The colonel complained of being separated from his own men and being placed over others who neither knew him nor his voice. We had now advanced more than half round the ramparts, and were quite at a loss to account for not having seen or heard anything of the other attacking columns so anxiously looked for. We had passed the Antwerp and were close upon the Breda Gate. At Bastion No 8 our progress was arrested by a more numerous body than we had hitherto encountered, who seemed determined to contest our further advance. This bastion was planted with trees, from behind which they fired upon us. Our party returned the fire.

Their ardour being damped, they were reluctant to come to the charge. We had, however, become mixed with them in hand to hand fight around the trees, and were making prisoners when the slow beat of a drum attracted our attention. As this ominous sound drew nearer our opponents took fresh courage, while it filled us with anxiety. We soon discerned a large body of men advancing with measured step along the curtain leading to the bastion in which we were engaged. Our contest was renewed with fresh energy. A ball felled General Gore, which I noticed to Colonel Carleton. The column still gradually and cautiously approached with the same ominous beat of drum, until they had entered to the middle of the bastion, when they came to a halt as if to discern between friends and foes.

This gave our brave colonel an opportunity of rallying his little band, and the prisoners in our rear concealed in some measure the insignificance of our numbers. Observing their hesitation (for a sort of solemn pause had taken place), our gallant colonel put on a bold face and stepping in advance said, '*Messieurs, mettez bas vos armes.*' The answer was a volley of musketry, and this distinguished officer fell to the ground.

Our party now made a simultaneous movement in retreat, but finding that after a little firing the column resumed its former caution with slow step and beat of drum, we retired leisurely with the hope of falling in with our own people. (After Carleton's death Sperling himself conducted the retiring movement.) This cautious advance and hesitation of the main body of the garrison proceeded probably from the supposition that we were merely a detachment preceding the main body. It, however, proved our safety and enabled us to bring off our prisoners, as we met with no opposition except from stragglers, who had resorted to the ramparts. When we had retired to about the place where the advance had been sounded in our previous progress, we discerned a large body of men in front of us.

We anxiously hailed them. They, knowing that no column had entered in the direction from which we came, had so entirely concluded us enemies, and were prepared to treat us as such that no response was made to our cry. Imagine our mutual joy when we recognised each other, and found that this was Major-General Cooke's column, consisting principally of the (Guards, which had effected its entrance by the *bâtardeau*. The other column, which attempted an entrance near the Breda Gate, the next bastion to the one where we met our repulse, had been obliged to retire with considerable loss, and were brought in following the Guards.

With General Cooke I had the pleasure of falling in with Colonel Smyth and Sir G. Hoste, and exchanging mutual congratulations, considering that the place was ours, but was sorry to hear that Abbey was shot through the leg and arm (he now lies in a doubtful state—the wounds proved fatal), and Adamson (the Sub-Lieut. of the Company of Royal Sappers and Miners), killed by a shot through the head. The opinion of our leaders was that we should remain quiet during the night and take possession in the morning. Colonel Smyth then took his leave to report to the General, Sir G. Hoste accompanying him.

Such is Sperling's narrative of the proceedings so far as they fell under his eye. It only remains to state that column B had found no difficulty in escalading and entering at the point designated for them under the guidance of Captain Sir George Hoste, R.E. Column C found the enemy prepared for their reception, and suffered some loss, amongst others Lieutenant Abbey, R.E., the guide, who was mortally wounded. Failing to penetrate at the intended point, they were drawn off and entered the fortress at the same spot as column B, to which they were joined, forming up on the left. Column D, allotted to the

SAPPER OF ROYAL ENGINEERS, 1813

false attack, did its work well, although it opened fire somewhat prematurely, and thus alarmed the garrison before the other columns had effected an entrance.

The idea was that by making as much demonstration as possible they would draw off the garrison from the real points of attack, and in this they were very successful, as the defenders were principally concentrated in the vicinity of the Steenburg Gate, their point of attack. Indeed, some of them must have actually penetrated within the works, although they were unprovided with ladders, as several were found killed on the ramparts near the gate.

Until now all had gone well. More than 2,500 men were within the place and in communication with their reserves outside. It required but a little promptitude and decision to complete what had hitherto been a brilliant success. From this time, however, every step taken appears to have been one of a series of mistakes. The first and most fatal error was the decision that the force should remain quiescent on the ramparts awaiting daylight without making any immediate attempt to secure its advantage; the second fault was that no effort was made to concentrate the troops forming column A.

The advance party of that column, under Colonel Carleton, had done all that was wanted, as described by Sperling, who guided them. The next portion of the column had unaccountably turned to the left and become enclosed within two bastions, whilst the river, now no longer fordable owing to the rise of the tide, cut them off from their comrades. The remainder had been posted in the outwork, apparently with the idea of securing the Water Gate. General Skerret, who commanded the force, had been killed, and no one seems to have been in a position to take his place. The two next officers to him. General Gore and Colonel Carleton, had both also been killed, and the column, divided as it was into three separate detachments, was practically without leaders.

The third error was the detaching a battalion from the main body to assist and support the party at the Water Gate, thus further weakening the force required to secure the place. Such was the position of affairs when day broke. The garrison had by that time recovered from their surprise, and finding that no effort had been made by the enemy to complete the capture of the town, they themselves pushed forward to the attack in the endeavour to recover the advantage they had lost in the assault.

The party enclosed in the two bastions to the left of the Water Gate made a stubborn defence, but being completely cut off was before long compelled to surrender. The force at the Water Gate, augmented by the battalion that had been sent to its support, was now exposed to a heavy fire from the ramparts behind. Part retreated through the gate to the ground outside, and found themselves enclosed in a *cul de sac*. Being unable to escape they also surrendered. The remainder climbed over the ramparts and, crossing the ditch, succeeded in making good their retreat, with the loss, however, of many men who were drowned by the breaking of the ice. These calamities caused Sir T. Graham to order the withdrawal of the remainder of the troops and the abandonment of the enterprise. Thus, ended in disaster an operation which seemed to have been brilliantly conceived and dashingly executed. The extent of the calamity is well summed up by Colonel Carmichael Smyth in his notes on the subject:—

We were doomed to drink the bitter draught of mortification and disappointment to the very dregs. When we came to exchange our prisoners on the following day, we received from the enemy more British soldiers than there were efficient French troops in the fortress.

The following letter was addressed to Colonel Smyth by the Inspector-General of Fortifications on the subject:—

Pall Mall, 2nd April, 1814.

Sir,—Lieutenant-General Mann desires me to inform you that His Lordship the Master-General, before whom your report of the gallant, though unsuccessful, attack upon the fortress of Bergen-op-Zoom has been laid, has expressed himself highly satisfied with the zealous conduct of yourself and the officers of Engineers, as well as the officers, non-commissioned officers, and soldiers of the Royal Sappers and Miners on the above occasion. I am also desired to convey a particular approbation of the gallantry and ability shown by Lieutenant Sperling while attached to the advanced party which first entered the fortress under the immediate command of the late Colonel Carleton. You will be pleased to make known this communication to the officers and men under your orders.

I am, &c., &c.,

Signed,   John Rowley,
                      Dy. Inspr. Genl. of Fortifications.

April 2nd. Two additional captains of Engineers have joined us—Oldfield and Harris.

As a consequence of the conclusion of war by the abdication of Napoleon, the French were withdrawn from all the fortresses of the Low Countries, and Sperling thus records the taking over of Antwerp:—

2nd May, 1814. This morning I accompanied the commanding officers of Artillery and Engineers with the other officers of each corps into Antwerp. (Sperling had been appointed Adjutant, *vice* Abbey, killed at Bergen-op-Zoom.) We were attended also by the heads of the different departments with their staff. A selection was to be made of different officers to receive over the stores of their special department in Antwerp and the various forts occupied by the French, who, on their part, did the same, appointing officers to deliver them up. We made altogether a large cavalcade, and were welcomed by the inhabitants, who expressed their pleasure at our entrance . . . . . The French Commanding Engineer seemed an intelligent officer, and we had some pleasant converse. He said he would prefer defending Antwerp to any fortress in Europe. He expressed great surprise at our leaving Bergen-op-Zoom after having it in possession.

12th May. On account of the number of fortresses to be occupied, there has been a considerable increase in the number of R. E. officers, and another company of sappers. It has been thought desirable to arrange a mess at an hotel instead of dining as we now do, subject to their charges. The price paid is three *francs* a day.

This entry is somewhat puzzling, as, at the date when it was made, only two additional Engineers had joined, *viz.*, Second Captains Oldfield and Harris, in June, July, and August, the following six were added:—Captain Sir C. F. Smith, and Lieutenants Cole, Covey, Kay, Mackenzie, and Ker.

Matters remained quiet in Holland and Belgium for the rest of the year, and arrangements were being made for the gradual transfer of all the strong places to the Dutch. Early in 1815 all was changed. We get a glimpse of the excitement that prevailed from Sperling's *Journal:*—

March 13th, 1815. Intelligence of Buonaparte's escape from Elba and landing in France reached us on the 9th. On the 10th, Major Tylden, R.E., dined with me.

March 14th. White arrived from England. . . . The report of Buonaparte's rapid and successful progress has put us all on the alert. General alarm is the consequence. . . . . . Should he continue his progress in this country our retreat may be as rapid as it was in '94, for though we have several fortresses, yet it is a work of time to provision and put them into a state to resist an attack. In making too large a grasp, we may lose that which, otherwise, we might have some hope of retaining. . . . . . Our officers are being distributed in the fortresses, and defensive preparations are being carried out.

29th March. I dined yesterday with the colonel. At his recommendation a brigade-major has been appointed to our department. He has chosen Captain Oldfield, who served under him in Scotland. We have all now our hands full of work.

By this time the strength of the Royal Engineers had been raised to thirty-one, and in the course of the following three months that number was increased to sixty.

31st March. We have reports of Buonaparte's advance.

On the following day Sperling was sent to Ghent to carry out works to cover the bridge over the Scheldt, and otherwise strengthen the town.

April 2nd. We commenced this morning with 250 men. They were set to construct two earthen redoubts, also to reinstate part of the town rampart which had quite lost its original shape. Besides myself, there were two junior officers of Engineers, and an Assistant Engineer from the Line. Our number of workmen increasing the next two days, they at last amounted to 2,000.

April 10th. The works being now in a forward state. Lieutenant Bolton was left in charge till the arrival of Captain Harris. I returned to Brussels. . . . . . I found the Duke of Wellington had been some days at Brussels.

April 12th. This day's post has brought the thanks of the master-general for our exertions in putting the fortresses into an efficient state.

April 13th. From the great increase of the department, we muster now about 50 officers with a very good field equipment, pontoon train, &c. The heads of departments are now somewhat anxious as to their positions, the duke having made so many changes in Spain on taking the command. There is an apprehension of the same now. It is also said that Colonel Burgoyne and the Peninsular Engineer officers who served under the duke in the Spanish sieges expect to occupy Colonel Smyth's position.

June 13th, Sir George Hoste has joined us from England, and we are still looking for more officers. Though headquarters continue at Brussels, the prospect of our moving seems approaching. Many seem to have very sanguine expectations of a speedy termination to the contest.

This last entry proved a very faithful foresight, as Napoleon's brief inroad into Belgium was close at hand, the Battle of Waterloo being fought five days later. The following Engineer officers were present on the field:—Lieutenant-Colonel James Carmichael Smyth, C.R.E.; Captains Sir George Charles Hoste, John Oldfield, Brigade Major; Second Captains Frank Stanway, Alexander Thomson, John William Pringle; Lieutenants Marcus Antonius Waters, Francis Bond Head, Francis Yarde Gilbert, John Sperling (Adjutant), and Andrew Douglas White.

June 17th. Major Oldfield and myself were ordered to join the colonel this morning (they had been left behind at Brussels when the army first advanced, and were not present at Quatre Bras). This relieved us from the suspense and anxiety of the preceding day. On reaching the army we found the retreat had commenced, rendered necessary by the defeat of the Prussians, that our connection with them might be maintained. It was a beautiful sight in an open country to see the cavalry and light troops retiring from hill to hill, while the infantry, thus protected, were withdrawing by the road in good order. . . . . . Soon after I reached the army the duke desired the colonel to have an entrenchment at Brain-le-Leud, which was to form a protection on the right of the intended position.
There was a company of sappers at Hal. I was accordingly di-

rected to proceed thither, and order them to march immediately to Brain-le-Leud to make an entrenchment. My first thought was to shorten the distance by traversing the forest of Soigny, but I soon saw that from waterways and cross paths I should get into difficulty, therefore hastening to Brussels I got a fresh horse, for the one I rode had been out all day. Through pouring rain Hal was reached by five o'clock. Having communicated the colonel's direction to the captain, the company was ordered for marching at six o'clock. I returned to Brussels and slept there."

June 18th. Left Brussels early in the morning. Joined some officers of Artillery on the road. Arriving at Waterloo, found Sir G. Hoste and Oldfield at their billet breakfasting, whom I joined. The colonel was with the duke, inspecting the position which had been taken up. . . . When the colonel returned to the village, he was displeased that the duke had not found the company of sappers at Brain-le-Leud, which arrived soon after at Waterloo. It appeared that, though the distance was about seven miles, from the intricacy of the lanes through the forest, they had missed the way that inclement night, and lost themselves in the forest.

Such is Sperling's account of this transaction. The Brigade-Major, Captain Oldfield, wrote also a diary of the events of this important campaign, and he throws a slightly different light on the affair. He is writing of the morning of June 18th:—

Soon after Col. Smyth had left, Captain —— (the name is nowhere given) came in and told me that he was in arrest by the colonel, who, it seems, had met him at the entrance of the village (of Waterloo), whither he had come in place of remaining at Braine-le-leud; that he had proceeded to the town of Braine-le-leud, and hearing from the major that British troops had left it the preceding day, he moved his people forward to Waterloo, which he considered as part of the position, and was looking about when Col. Smyth came up. . . . . The error of the captain, who disliked being in the rear and was anxious to see what was doing in the front, might have led to the most unfortunate results had we experienced any reverse.

This company was the First of the Fourth Battalion, and seems to have been all through most unfortunate. Having failed to construct the intrenchment by which the duke had intended to strengthen his right, it remained in front of the village of Waterloo during the best part of the 18th. Towards afternoon, Sir George Hoste ordered it to fall back, and it was moved to the rear of the village. At this time Lieutenants W. Faris and C. K. Sanders, R.E., and Sub-lieutenant R. Turner were with it, the captain being in arrest in the village of Waterloo. In the position the company had taken up it blocked the road, and when the Belgians and Hanoverians, struck with panic, were retiring hastily, they carried away the company of sappers with them.

Lieutenant Sanders being informed by the fugitives that the French were close at hand, and that the road for retreat would shortly be intercepted, unfortunately permitted his men to join in the tumultuous stream. There is no doubt that everyone concerned behaved badly. The men lost their knapsacks; tools, baggage, and horses were also abandoned, and the company was thoroughly disorganised. As a consequence. Colonel Smyth refused to recommend any of the officers or men attached to it for the Waterloo honours and advantages.

Having faithfully narrated this unfortunate blot on the general good service of the corps, we will give a different account of the conduct of another company from Oldfield's *Journal*:—

> A company of sappers arrived from Antwerp at Bruxelles on the morning of the 18th. The sub-lieutenant immediately proceeded to the office, ascertained that Captain Stanway, who was appointed to the command, was with the army, and proceeded at once with his company to place himself under orders, making his way from Bruxelles to Waterloo through hosts of fugitives and impediments, regardless of the reports of the fate of the day having gone against us. They arrived on the field unfortunately too late to participate in the action.

During the action of the 18th Oldfield records:—

> In another of the charges, Lord Uxbridge rode up to Colonel Smyth and expressed his desire to get some guns to bear upon the enemy, who were coming down upon us in great force. Upon which the colonel offered my services to Lord Uxbridge, by whose directions I went in search of some guns, and falling in with two moving in rear of our first line, brought them up at a trot to Lord Uxbridge, who gave them further directions.

He gives the following interesting particulars about a plan of the position of Waterloo:—

Shortly after my chief had joined headquarters (this was on the 16th) he sent in to me for the plan of the position of Waterloo, which had been previously reconnoitred. The several sketches of the officers had been put together, and one fair copy made for the Prince of Orange. A second had been commenced in the drawing-room for the duke, but was not in a state to send, I therefore forwarded the original sketches of the officers.

(*Morning of the 17th.*) Upon my joining Col. Smyth, he desired me to receive from Lieut. Waters the plan of the position, which, according to his desire, I had sent to him from Bruxelles the preceding day, and of which I was told to take the greatest care. It had been lost in one of the charges of the French cavalry and recovered. Lieut. Waters, who had it in his cloak before his saddle (or in his sabretache attached to his saddle, I forgot which), was unhorsed in the *mêlée* and ridden over. Upon recovering himself, he found the cavalry had passed him, and his horse was nowhere to be seen. He felt alarmed for the loss of his plan. To look for his horse he imagined was in vain, and his only care was to avoid being taken prisoner, which he hoped to do by keeping well towards our right.

The enemy being repulsed in his charge was returning by the left to the ground from which he had advanced. After proceeding about fifty yards, he was delighted to find his horse quietly destroying the vegetables in a garden near the farmhouse at Quatre Bras. He thus fortunately recovered his plan, and with it rejoined the colonel. The retreat of the Prussians upon Wavre rendered it necessary for the duke to make a corresponding movement, and upon the receipt of a communication from Blücher, he called Col. Smyth and asked him for his plan of the position of Waterloo, which I immediately handed to him. The duke then gave directions to Sir William de Lancy to put the army in position at Waterloo, forming them across the Nivelles and Charleroi *chaussées*.

We will now once more take up Sperling's account:—

Being with the colonel, who accompanied the duke with his staff in the early part of the battle, until by the various charges we became scattered, seeking refuge in the infantry squares, but remaining on the hill near the artillery, the best opportunity was afforded of seeing the battle. Sometimes we were enveloped in smoke, shells bursting on all sides, cannon balls and bullets flying about. Nevertheless, every movement was effected with that order and precision which excited admiration even in such a terrific scene of desolation, in which were continually multiplying the dead and dying. Horses were galloping about, having lost their riders; others were maimed. Wounded men were limping or creeping to the rear; others, more severely, were being assisted. . . . . The infantry were drawn up in two lines of squares, flanking each other, on the slope of the hill, a little retired from the summit, so as to be completely under cover, yet able to act as occasion might require, and capable of resisting any attack of cavalry.

Skirmishing parties were in advance, and on the flanks. . . . . Hugomont was the scene of animated contest and great loss of life; but wo kept possession of it, or rather what remained of it. La Haye Sainte was subject to a similar contest; but there, I believe, we were not so successful. . . . . During the battle I was sent with a message to Waterloo. (Probably this was the message to the company of sappers to retire behind the village.) If order prevailed in the battlefield there was the greatest confusion in the rear. Some recruits, Belgian cavalry, I believe, had taken fright, and spread the report that the battle was lost. Brussels was filled with alarm, and the road to it with confusion. . . . . Pringle of ours is wounded in the breast; I hope not dangerously. A bullet through the elbow of my coat, and another on my saddle, have reminded me of my gracious Preserver. . . . . . We paused some time on the battlefield. The colonel, thoughtful of some memorial, dismounted and took up an officer's sword from the slain. It did not occur to me to do the same, nor did I think how soon the spoilers would be over the dead.

The night coming on, we returned to Waterloo with light hearts. On reaching the morning's billet, we found it turned into a hospital filled with the wounded, and presenting a melancholy sight. A vacant room was, however, obtained in the village, which accommodated all the Engineer subalterns, about eight in number. We got some food, and the ready wit of Francis Bond Head, who was one of those so nearly taken by the French at Charleroi, escaping without his hat, told so effectually on our host that he supplied us with wine. After this most of us wrote a few lines to our friends to accompany the despatches. For the night we laid down upon some straw, with our feet to the centre of the room.

Sir John Jones, in his autobiographical *Memoir*, has the following interesting details. He was accompanying the duke in their annual inspection of the Netherland fortresses in 1819, and on passing the field of Waterloo the duke walked over it with him, and explained all the leading features of the battle. Jones has noted the following points:—

Speaking of the quality of his army he said, 'I had only about 35,000 men on whom I could thoroughly rely; the remainder were but too likely to run away.' He mentioned, in proof of the latter assertion, that the Belges, before the battle commenced, were placed along the hedge on the left of the *chaussée*, and the division of General Picton and Kempt's and Pack's brigades were posted in reserve on the extreme left. The Belges, on the very first forward movement of the French, all quitted their ground, and he was obliged to occupy it with two divisions from the extreme left, so that no reserve existed on that point, which damaged all his plans, and sadly diminished his means of resistance where the French made their most strenuous exertions. Coupled with this, his plans wore sadly deranged by the conduct of a general of the Hanoverian Landwehr, on whom the command of the troops devolved on Baron Alten being wounded.

The force posted on this point consisted of a British brigade, a brigade of the German Legion, and two brigades of Hanoverians, and instantly, on the fall of Alten, General ——, without saying a word to the duke, retired his division from its advanced position, and removed to the rear. La Haye Sainte had just fallen, and the duke came to the spot to make a fresh disposition of the troops in its rear, with a view to parry the effects of its loss, when, to his amazement, he found them all gone, and was received by a fire from the French *tirailleurs* from the very ground on which he had posted, and still expected to find the division, thus marched away. It was now in consequence of these two withdrawals with the utmost difficulty that he could collect men sufficient even to spread over the ground, and the misbehaviour of this militia general had well-nigh cost him the battle.

At another period of the action, having ordered up the Nassau troops, they fell into confusion and gave way, and when he went personally to rally them and induce them to move forward, they absolutely fired at him. 'In fact,' said the duke, 'there was so much misbehaviour that it was only through God's mercy that we won the battle.' These were his very words noted a few minutes after their being uttered.

Colonel Jones having asked him whether he did not think that the French fought better than in Spain, owing to being commanded by their emperor in person, he replied, "I saw no difference in our hard fought actions here and there. If I had had the same army as in the south of France the battle would have been won in three hours." The duke continued:—

I first saw the Prussian videttes about half-past two, and never in my life did I observe a movement with such intense interest; the time they occupied in approaching us seemed interminable—both they and my watch seemed to have stuck fast.

Colonel Jones adds to his account:—

During their walk over the position, the celebrated guide De Coster and a set of ragged urchins kept offering for sale buttons, bullets, and all sorts of trash picked up on the field, and would insist on enforcing on the duke their own version of the battle. This he bore with perfect equanimity and good humour, till being interrupted whilst giving a most interesting account of the steadiness of the infantry in opposing the cavalry, by a ridiculous rhodomontade as to his own individual conduct, he said sharply in French, 'Allow me to know what I did myself;' to which Colonel Jones added, 'This is the Duke of Wellington.' At this announcement they all appeared to be petrified, stared with astonishment for a few moments, and then followed at a respectful distance till they regained the carriage.

In the year 1816, Colonel Jones was invited to dine with Sir George Murray in Paris to meet General Foy, and the conversation turned on Waterloo. Foy said on that occasion:—

The emperor sent for me about 10 a.m., and accosted me thus: '*Monsieur le Général*, you have often fought the English; here is their rear guard, and we shall have a *jolie affaire* with them if they wait an hour longer. What will they do?' 'Pardon me, Sire, if I say that I believe Wellington's whole army is here; the English troops keep quiet and out of sight till the attacking columns are close to them, then they jump up and advance, and are as steady and fit to act as if they had been from the first in line. I humbly conceive that such will prove to be the case today.' '*Non, non.* There is nothing here but a rear guard, and we shall have a very *jolie affaire.*'

Sir John Burgoyne paid a visit to the field of Waterloo in 1816, and after a careful inspection of the ground, wrote an able paper on the subject of the battle. The following extract on the Engineer side of the question may be read with interest:—

Even a single company of sappers, with their tools, might in a very few hours have rendered most essential service in improving it (our ground), by preparing the two buildings for defence, and throwing up traverses for guns across the two *chaussées*. The Guards did to the *château* what was necessary for its defence. Had the Haye Sainte been loopholed, all its doors and approaches towards the front and flanks been strongly barricaded, and a communication made to the rear, it would probably have been held through the whole day. The traverse across the Genappe *chaussée* would have given our artillery the command of that road by which the enemy brought down his troops to many of the most serious attacks, and still more so, had the eighteen-pounders been up which had been prepared for the field. Had there been opportunity and means for more work, the points are clearly marked out where four or six detached works might have been placed to advantage, besides the cover that might be thrown up for the line.

The duke did not wish to have any ground entrenched which might give any clue to his intentions, but would have been glad to have had anything which could be thrown up at the time. Two companies of sappers and 3,000 men might, on the night of the 17th, in addition to the above-mentioned posts, have thrown up such a line as would have afforded great cover to our infantry and guns, have brought them more to the ridge of the hill, and would have considerably checked and broken the advances of cavalry.

Immediately after the victory of Waterloo, the British and Prussian Armies advanced into France on their road to Paris. Cambray capitulated without a shot; but at Péronne the *commandant* refused to surrender, and arrangements were made for an assault. This fortress, which is on the Somme, has powerful fronts to the north and east on the land side, and is protected on the other two sides by the river. The eastern front is covered by a large horn-work, with a ravelin before it, the whole enclosed with glacis and covert way. It was ascertained that there was no drawbridge, the entrance being closed by massive gates.

Two columns were told off—one to escalade the right bastion of the horn-work; the other, with two guns, to blow in the gate and enter through the ravelin. Two brigades of guns were to cover the operation, one to sweep the faces of the horn-work, the other to enfilade the main front behind it, so as to prevent the garrison on that point from bringing their fire on the assailants when they had entered the advanced work. The attack was perfectly successful. The garrison, evidently cowed by the French disasters and the ignominious capitulation of Cambray, made a very half-hearted defence; and as soon as the British had established themselves in the horn-work they surrendered the fortress.

The Second Company of the Second Battalion of Sappers had the honour of leading the assaulting columns; one portion being with the ladders for the escalade, the remainder with the column that was to enter by the gateway. Sub-Lieutenant Stratton and Lance-Corporal Edward Connall clambered over the gate, forced their way through the spikes, and jumped into the work. They then tore down the fastenings and admitted the troops. (Conolly: *History of the Royal Sappers and Miners*, vol 1.) This was after the fire of the guns had much injured the structure. Captain Thomson, R.E., led the escalade at the bastion. Both he and Stratton were severely wounded. This took place on June 26th, and a Dutch garrison was left in the place.

Sperling's *Journal.*—

June 28th. I was despatched with a message to the officer placed in command at Péronne, and to make observations with respect to the fortifications and their state. I arrived there about 10 o'clock. The governor kindly insisted on my breakfasting, or rather taking lunch with him and some of his officers. On my showing some surprise at the abundance of his table, he said that as the French had almost ruined them, they were now living at free quarters; the inhabitants furnished what they required. I afterwards rode round the fortifications. They are so strong that our getting possession arose only from the weakness and hesitation of its defenders.

Meanwhile, the Engineer force with the army had been distributed in accordance with a corps order, issued by Colonel Smyth on June 20th. A brigade of Engineers was attached to each division. This brigade consisted of a captain, three subalterns, and a company of sappers under its sub-lieutenant, with drivers, horses, and waggons, carrying intrenching tools for the employment of 500 men, also a due equipment of artificers' tools and other stores. The pontoon train consisted of four companies, afterwards augmented to five, carrying eighty pontoons, besides store waggons, &c., for the transport of which 800 horses were attached. This train was under the command of Major Tylden, R.E. At this time the Engineer establishment, either with the army or in the various fortresses in the Netherlands, consisted of 60 officers, 10 Companies of sappers, with 550 drivers, 1,000 horses, and about 160 waggons of various kinds.

The lesson had at length been thoroughly learnt that an army requires for its efficient service a complete Engineer equipment. After having suffered severely from the want of such assistance in the Peninsula, the evil had at last been remedied. Unfortunately, the long peace which followed the close of the French war led the authorities to forget the experience that had been so dearly bought. When once again England became involved in a great European struggle, her Engineer equipment was not much better than it had been in the early days of the Peninsular War. The sole exception was that of the men, of whom it possessed a body whose training left but little to be desired. These were, however, sadly hampered for want of the due provision of *matériel* and transport.

Sperlings *Journal*,—

2nd July. Sent to Major Tylden, who commands the pontoon train at Sarcelles, directing him to select the best places for throwing bridges over the Seine. The bridges had been rendered impassable by the French, excepting at St. Germains, where a great part of the Prussian Army had crossed to take Paris on the south. St. Denis and Montmartre, to the north, have been strongly intrenched, so that any attack from the north, where we are, would be very destructive. Returned to Gonesse in the evening. My ride proved a long one, having to visit three places along the Seine—Argenteuil, Besons and Carnères, to enable me to speak as to their eligibility for the bridge. From our proximity to St. Denis, and the uncertainty of things, we are obliged to be continually on the alert The colonel gratified me yesterday with the intelligence he had received of his being appointed *aide-de-camp* to the Prince Regent; the more flattering, as it is the first appointment that has been made from our corps. It gives him the rank of Colonel.

It may be mentioned here that Colonel Carmichael Smyth was made a baronet, and received the K.C.B., for his services in this campaign, as well as the A.D.C.-ship here referred to.

Argenteuil was the site selected for the bridge, a second one being also established at Asnières. These bridges were maintained for several months, being made movable in the centre to admit of the navigation being unimpeded. The army entered Paris on July 8th, and the war terminated.

Meanwhile, Lieutenant-Colonel Burgoyne, who had landed at Ostend on July 6th, was pushing forward to join the army, but was too late for any of its active operations. On the 15th he reached Péronne, where he found the same Dutch *commandant* who had been so hospitable to Sperling, and who appears to have been equally so to him. He records that this colonel had received his first commission on the recommendation of Lord Macdonald, of the British Guards, at Linselles, in 1793, and that after serving in the French Army under Napoleon for several years, including the campaign in Russia, he joined the Dutch Army, under the Prince of Orange, on the abdication of the French Emperor in 1814. He was present at Waterloo, where Sir Thomas Picton, a few minutes before he was killed, tapped him on the shoulder, saying, "*Brave Hollandais, Ferme.*"

These two compliments from British generals had rendered him a complete Anglomaniac, hence his overflowing hospitalities to British officers, of which Burgoyne and Sperling derived the benefit.

Alter a residence in Paris of some months, Burgoyne was appointed, on December 9th, commissioner on the part of the Duke of Wellington to proceed to Mézières and Sédan, where, conjointly with Colonel Adye, of the Artillery, he was to take over these fortresses, and transfer them to the charge of the Prussians, who were to hold them during the occupation. Much dispute arose with the Prussians as regarded the artillery, ammunition, and stores, which they considered had become their property, and were not to be restored to the French when the places were given back. The brass guns had already been sent off to Prussia, when Burgoyne arrived; but there were 100 iron guns, with their carriages, and a large quantity of stores, that had not yet started.

The discussions on this point were so prolonged that it was not until April 6th, 1816, that the transfer was effected, and the inventories signed.

Lieutenant-Colonel Jones having recovered from the severe wound he had received at Burgos, although still somewhat lame and unfitted for active exertion, had in 1814 visited the principal fortresses on the Netherlands frontier in order to make a careful inspection of their strength and equipment. Having completed this, he pushed on to Paris, where he found the Duke of Wellington, who had arrived to take part in the first occupation. The duke at once named him as one of a commission of Engineers, to report upon the increase and development of those fortresses that would be necessary in order to render the frontier of the new kingdom of Holland secure.

The return of Napoleon from Elba, and the consequent war, had prevented any action being taken at the time. Now, however, that peace was again restored, the British commission commenced its functions. The officers composing it were General Bryce, Colonel Carmichael Smyth, and Lieutenant-Colonel Jones. At the same time a commission of Dutch Engineers was also named, consisting of General Croiset, Colonel Vanderkyck, and Major Valter. These two bodies acted quite independently of each other, and submitted separate reports and estimates of what services they considered necessary. Those of the British were completed in August, 1815, the Dutch papers following shortly after.

The Duke of Wellington, with whom rested the ultimate decision in the matter, studied the two reports most carefully. As Colonel Jones has recorded in his *Memoir* on this subject—

The Commission was in constant communication with the Duke of Wellington, who, notwithstanding the numerous and important calls on his time, frequently gave up two hours consecutively to discuss the various projects for defence brought before him; and this he did not superficially and in the mass, but entered most minutely into every consideration, whether professional, strategic, or financial.

The English report and estimate provided for strengthening the

151

following points:—

Places.	No. of Garrison.	Calculated Time of Defence—Days.	Estimated Cost.	Time to Complete—Years.
			£	
Nieuport	3,000	30 to 32	115,784	3
Ypres	5,000	32	153,561	3
Redoubt at Merrin ..	300	6 to 7	39,925	3
Courtray	6,000	32 to 34	457,579	7
Tournay { Town	1,500	8 to 10	78,391	2
Tournay { Citadel	3,500	30 to 32	87,835	2
Oudenarde	2,500	16	190,128	4
Citadel of Ghent	1,800	10	50,975	2
Dendermonde	3,500	34 to 36	230,670	5
Ostend	5,000	36	125,507	3
Antwerp	8,000	32	49,386	2
Grammont	2,500	18	167,256	4
Ath	3,000	22 to 24	143,599	3
Mons	6,000	34 to 36	380,288	7
Redoubts at Binche	600	5 to 6	50,000	2
Charleroy	4,500	26	188,123	4
Citadel of Namur	4,000	28 to 30	117,135	3
New Work at Huy	2,500	26	170,000	4
Liège	2,500	20	120,000	4
			£2,916,142	
To which 10 per cent. was added for contingencies ..			291,614	
			£3,207,756	

The Dutch report and estimate did not include all the points that were embraced in that of the British; but, on the other hand, their estimates were higher for those they did report on.

The ultimate result was, that a scheme of defence was sanctioned, containing some of the details brought forward by each commission; the British report having been in the main adopted, but modified in many points, where the duke preferred the suggestions of the Dutch.

The revised estimate then stood thus:—

Original British estimate ..   £3,207,756
Purchase of land, and other details   800,000
Additional cost of adopting Dutch proposals—
At Ypres, an excess of   £28,000
  " Ath   "   "   266,000
  " Ostend "   "   329,000
  " Antwerp "   "   176,000
  " Maestrecht, not included at
    all in the British scheme   222,000
                               ————————
                                                1,021,000
                                                ————————

Carried forward £5,028,756

152

Brought forward £5,028,756	
For the town of Namur	120,000
Brussels	120,000
For posts of observation between Nieuport	
and Ypres, proposed in Dutch project	140,000
Redoubt in front of Courtray	120,000
Two new fortresses in front of Brussels	
proposed by the Duke of Wellington	1,000,000
	£6,528,756

There were savings to the amount of £330,000, which were intended to be applied to the arming of the fortresses. The funds for this grand scheme were to be found as follows: England contributed two millions sterling, and Holland a similar amount, whilst two and a-half millions were to be taken from the contributions levied in France. By a convention signed between Great Britain and Holland, in November, 1816, the Duke of Wellington was appointed the disposer of this fund, with entire control over the details of construction of the various works embraced in the project. He was authorised to appoint under himself as many inspectors as he might think necessary to supervise the work, which was to be carried out by the Dutch Engineer department.

He, however, declined to have anyone under him but Colonel Jones, whom he named his sole assistant. The commissions were then broken up, and the construction of the works begun. This lasted from 1816 to 1828. During all that time Colonel Jones made frequent inspections and reports to the duke on the progress effected, and the duke himself annually travelled round the frontier in company with Jones, carefully looking into every detail.

Colonel Jones, in his autobiographical *memoir*, quotations from which have already been extracted, gives a very interesting description of these trips, during which he was thrown in constant and intimate contact with the duke. The revolution of 1830 rendered null all the efforts that had been made, and the Dutch lost the frontier which had been strengthened at so much cost.

As soon as it appeared likely that they would encounter difficulties in their Belgian provinces, the Duke of Wellington, who was at the time Prime Minister, sent for Colonel Jones, and entrusted him with a private mission to the King of Holland. The duke's words, as recorded by Jones, were:—

> I wish you to go over there and use your discretion as to any
> military arrangements that may become advisable, with a view
> to parry any threatened or probable hostile movements of the
> French; but be very guarded not to do anything to commit us
> or the Dutch; to ensure this, it is better you should see what I
> have written as to the determination of the English Govern-
> ment.

The narrative continues:—

> The day being damp and chilly, there was a fire in the room,
> and His Grace, placing his feet on the hob, and making Colonel
> Jones draw in and place his feet on the fender, then read to him
> his several confidential letters on the subject. Their substance
> may be stated in a few lines—that Great Britain would not in-
> terfere with the internal proceedings of France, but that she was
> bound by treaties to protect the Netherlands and her other al-
> lies, and that she was prepared and determined to do so on any
> aggressive movement of the French beyond their own frontier.
> After having ceased to read, the duke said, 'Now you know
> everything. Go round the frontier, recommend whatever you
> consider desirable for security, and I feel sure I can trust you to
> do whatever is right and expedient without compromising us.'

Armed with these instructions, Colonel Jones proceeded to the
Hague, where he was presented to the King of Holland by the British
Ambassador, Sir Charles Bagot. The king requested him to join the
headquarters of his son, the Prince of Orange, who was assembling a
force at Antwerp, to march on Brussels, where the popular ferment
was at its height, adding "*Mon Général* (such was the rank he gave
him), I have the highest confidence in your judgement and discretion.
Go to my sons, be their adviser, and I will write an order that your
opinion shall be asked and followed, as to any operations the army
may undertake."

Colonel Jones joined the Royal Princes at Antwerp, and marched
with them to Vilvorde, the troops consisting of 4,000 men, with twelve
guns. Here they were met by deputies from Brussels, who desired that
the Prince of Orange should enter that city without his troops, and
trust himself to the *burgher* guard. This, after some discussion, he agreed
to do, provided they would parade outside the town without wearing

the tricolour (the badge of the revolution), and further pledge themselves to obey his orders. "I will do this, he added, '*foi de Prince.*'"

When this decision had been communicated to the general staff, they all, being Dutch, strove to persuade him to abandon the idea, assuring him that he was not justified in incurring the risk, and that he was not bound to keep faith with men in active rebellion. The prince began to falter, and asked Colonel Jones his opinion. His reply was:—

> The word of honour of a prince is a sacred pledge, and I consider you are bound to meet the *Garde* tomorrow and enter Brussels under their escort.

In this the prince concurred, and the entry was made as arranged.

When, however, Jones endeavoured to persuade him to mollify the inhabitants by the removal of some real grievances, his Dutch surroundings, who were opposed to any concessions, were too powerful, and prevented any changes being proposed. Finding that he could be of no further use, and being doubtful how far his present position might compromise the British Government, he returned to England to report the state of affairs in person. Within two hours of his departure from Brussels the prince left the town, all the advantage of his presence there was lost, and in a short time Belgium had become severed from Holland.

One more point with reference to this matter is interesting, and is thus recorded by Jones:—

> Much intercourse with Lord Palmerston on the affairs of the Netherlands led Colonel Jones to form a very high opinion of his lordship's talents, and also of his honour and fair dealing, and that he only wanted capable instruments to become the zealous and judicious advocate of British interests, as the following incident will serve to explain. At one interview he desired Colonel Jones's opinion on a list of the names of six of the recently-constructed fortresses, which he had received from the French Government, as being those they proposed to raze under an agreement recently concluded to that effect.
> Colonel Jones instantly saw that the places selected were those which threw open the Belgian frontier, and those preserved were such as strengthened the French frontier, and expressed very strongly his dissent from the selection, and hoped it would receive further consideration. His Lordship replied: 'The destruction of these places is merely a sop to soothe the vanity of

the French people, and there can be no motive for the selection.' 'If so, My Lord, and you will give me leave, I will bring the matter to a fair test. Propose to substitute the following six places for destruction instead of those in this list; if the French have no unfair or aggressive views, they will readily give their consent to leave those places entire which are indispensable to the security of Belgium.'

Lord Palmerston readily adopted the suggestion; a counter list of six fortresses to be destroyed was sent back as being those only which he would consent to give up. On this decision being communicated to the French Government, a Council of War was held at Paris (the proceedings of which unaccountably found their way into the newspapers), in which it was decided it would be better for France not to destroy any fortress than those pointed out, and if they could not enforce their own list, they should wait for a more favourable moment to attain their object. Lord Palmerston was as firm as a rock, and to this day (notwithstanding the agreement to serve French vanity), the line of the Belgian frontier fortresses remains intact.

A History of the Sappers and Miners During the Period Covered by Sperling's Narrative

By T. W. J. Connolly

The Fourth company Second Battalion, counting eighty-two men, with Sub-Lieutenant T. Adamson under Captain R. Thomson, left Margate with the expedition under Sir Thomas Graham, and landed at Williamstadt the 18th December, 1813. There the company suffered loss by the accidental burning of the barracks in which it was quartered. After removing the stores from the shipping, parties were employed in preparing fascines and gabions, in bridge-making, constructing a landing place of faggots for the disembarkation of the cavalry, and in removing the platforms and heavy mortars from the ramparts at Williamstadt for carriage to Merxam.

These services being accomplished, the company was distributed to Klundert, Groat Zundert, Zandaarbuiten, Tholen, Steenbergen, and Fort Frederic near Lillo. Among other duties, the detachment at Zandaarbuiten formed, in a very expeditious manner, a bridge of country-boats over the River Maerk under two young lieutenants of engineers, which served for the conveyance of the heaviest artillery. The boats were of different shapes and sizes, collected for the occasion, and the materials for the superstructure were of irregular scantling, partly collected in the neighbourhood and partly felled on the spot. (Pasley's *Elementary Fortification*, 1.)

At Tholen a corporal and eight men under Lieutenant Eyre, R.E., attached to the Prussians, built a battery on the bank of the river for the protection of a flying bridge; and at Fort Frederic a party restored a battery for two guns, which afterwards held an unequal contest with a French eighty-four gun ship, and prevented her proceeding to

Bergen-op-Zoom with provisions. No less than forty-one, including the commander, were killed and wounded on board the man-of-war, while the casualties at the battery only amounted to one killed and two wounded.

Leaving sixteen men at Tholen and Zandaarbuiten, the remainder of the company, armed with short swords, felling axes, saws, &c., and guarding an establishment of mules drawing about one hundred waggons laden with intrenching tools, commenced the march for Antwerp. They followed the Royal Artillery, and reliefs of twenty men were, by turns, repeatedly ordered to the front to remove abattis and other obstructions that were met with on the route. From intense frost and a heavy and continuous fall of snow blowing in their faces, they encountered many difficulties and suffered extremely during the journey.

Merxam being taken on the 2nd February, the company and a strong force of the guards and line, began the erection of batteries to attack the fleet at Antwerp. By command, no relief was permitted to the sappers, and they continued on duty for seventy-two hours without intermission. Their steady labours at the Napoleon battery of sixteen guns, and their skill in revetting the embrasures, and in attending to the more perilous parts of the works, were the wonder of both officers and soldiers. Sir Thomas Graham, in general orders dated Merxam, 5th February, did full justice to the zeal and exertions of the sappers, and stated, "that they deserved the highest praise." Two privates were wounded.

Sergeant William Stevens and Corporal Thomas Milburn distinguished themselves by their coolness and bravery in superintending the laying of platforms and making a splinter proof magazine under a heavy fire. Recommended by Colonel Carmichael Smyth, the commanding Royal Engineer, the former was forthwith appointed colour-sergeant, and soon afterwards commissioned to a sub-lieutenancy in the corps; and the latter was promoted to be sergeant.

After the failure at Antwerp, the headquarters of the company went into cantonments at Rosendaal, and parties were detached to Groat Zundert, Fort Henrick, Calmthout, Eschen, and Brieschaet At Groat Zundert seven men under Corporal James Hilton conducted some experimental bridging in the presence of Sir Thomas Graham and Colonel Carmichael Smyth, with the view of adopting the easiest plan for crossing ditches in future enterprises. Sir Thomas was struck with the simplicity of the corporal's arrangement and the rapidity of its execution; and as a proof of his approbation gave him a *napoleon*.

Royal Sappers & Miners, working dress, 1813

On another occasion, that distinguished general took particular interest in the formation of a ditch bridge and even laboured himself in its construction. From the unevenness of the banks the baulks did not lie firmly. Private James McKay was in the act of obtaining the desired steadiness, when Sir Thomas took a spare spade, cut some sods, and assisting to place them in the required positions, only gave up when the work was satisfactorily accomplished.

In the surprise of Bergen-op-Zoom on the 8th March, parties of the company were attached to each of the columns appointed for the attack. There were about forty men in all, who were provided with axes, saws, and crowbars, and also a few ladders to scale the walls of the fortress. At about half-past ten o'clock the attack was made. The sappers cut down the palisades, crossed the ditches, planted the ladders, and leading the way in the escalade, were the first soldiers on the enemy's ramparts.

They then pushed forward to remove any obstacle that opposed the advance of the assailants, and persevered in their several duties till the place was captured. A reverse, however, awaited the British: the enemy renewed the attack with unwonted vigour, and in a few hours regained the fortress. During these extraordinary operations the following casualties occurred in the detachment: Sub-Lieutenant Adamson was killed by a cannon-ball on the glacis when advancing. About fifteen were wounded, of whom two mortally—privates John McKeer and James Munro, and ten others were taken prisoners, and conveyed to Fynaart, but shortly afterwards released.

Of the conduct of the sappers in this *coup-de-main* Colonel Carmichael Smyth has left it on record, that the company conducted themselves with the utmost coolness and courage, and the master-general, in a letter dated 2nd April, was pleased to express himself highly satisfied with the zealous conduct of the Royal Sappers and Miners on the above occasion.

The gallant behaviour of Corporal James Creighton and Private Edward Lomas is deserving of notice. After breaking through a palisade on the ramparts, they dashed forward and were challenged by a vigilant sentinel, who fired and shot Lomas in the thigh and then charged Creighton. Creighton parried the bayonet with his axe, and, seizing the Frenchman's musket, a desperate struggle ensued. The sentinel, who was a powerful man, at length threw his antagonist violently to the ground, and stamping his foot on his breast, endeavoured to wrest the firelock from the corporal's grasp. His strength spent, Creighton could scarcely maintain the contest, when Lomas, yet bleeding from his wound, rushed to the rescue of his comrade and struck the Frenchman with a pole-axe on the back of his head.

The blow was fatal. Lomas now armed himself with the musket and ammunition of the sentinel, and pressing forward into the fortress, his resolution and daring were further signalized by his killing two other Frenchmen, and wounding two more. The latter he delivered over as prisoners of war to sergeant Thomas Milburn of the company, first breaking their muskets in their presence, and then dispossessing them of their accoutrements.

★★★★★★★★★★

Lomas was discharged in 1816 by reduction, and being a young soldier, received no pension. Some forty years afterwards, he applied for a pension, and his exploits being still remembered, he was granted 6*d*. a day.

★★★★★★★★★★

Corporal Creighton followed Lomas in the adventure, but was too much fatigued and weakened to be of material service.

Soon after the reverse at Bergen-op-Zoom, the greater part of the company was sent to South Beveland and attached to the engineer brigades of Captain B. Thomson and Oldfield, to be employed in the attack of Fort Batz. The night that ground was to have been broken news arrived of peace. The company returned into cantonments at Rosendaal, then changed its headquarters to Horst, and in May assembled at Antwerp, where it remained, with the exception of some small detachments, to the end of the year. In July another company— Fourth of the Third Battalion—under Lieutenant P. Cole, arrived in that city from Woolwich. The strength of the sappers in the Netherlands was now 152.

The sub-lieutenants were James Adam and Edward Sanders. In September both companies were inspected at Brussels by Lieutenant-General Clinton, who expressed himself highly pleased with their appearance. For several months of the year the parties detached were employed at Liere, Schilde, Graven Wesel, Brussels, Tournay, and Mons.

To the force in Holland was added the Fifth company, Second Battalion, which embarked at Woolwich on the 2nd January, and landed at Antwerp the same month. This company and two others, already there, were employed for several months in improving the defences of the frontiers of the Netherlands, particularly at Ypres, Tournay, Mons, Dendermond, Ath, Namur, Charleroi, and Brussels. The various works were subdivided amongst the non-commissioned officers and privates, each of whom was held responsible for the proper execution of the work entrusted to his superintendence. The peasants and women under the direction of each counted from 20 to 100, and even more, according to circumstances. (Pasley's *Elementary Fortification*, 1.)

Sergeant John Purcell had from 300 to 400 women under his orders at Ypres; and from some winning peculiarity in his mode of command, obtained from their willing obedience and energies an amount of labour that was almost astonishing. No less than about 1,800 peasants and 2,000 horses were engaged in these works, and, by all accounts, they were conducted with the greatest regularity and dispatch. Sir Charles Pasley attributes no inconsiderable credit to the sappers for their assistance on the occasion; and the Master-General, the Earl of Mulgrave, in a letter dated 4th April, expressed his "warm approbation of their zeal and exertions."

Meanwhile Napoleon, breaking his captivity in Elba, reappeared in France, and, wherever he journeyed, was enthusiastically welcomed by his former legions. As by a spell, the army gathered under the wings of his eagles, and again lifted him into the imperial seat from which he had been so recently expelled. Europe was once more thrown into commotion by the event, and to crush the lofty hopes and pretensions of an intolerable ambition, war was at once declared by the Allies against the usurper.

At the instance of the Duke of Wellington, (Gurwood, 8), seven companies of the corps, instructed in their art, were hurried off to Ostend between the 24th March and 10th June, and distributed with all possible haste to those frontier posts and fortresses in the Netherlands that most required their services. Those companies were the:

Third and Sixth of the First Battalion;
Second and Eighth of the Second Battalion;
First and Seventh of the Third Battalion; and
First of the Fourth Battalion:

And they were employed in constructing indispensable fieldworks, or improving the fortifications at Ostend, Ghent, Nieuport, Tournay, Oudenarde, Boom, Escaneffe, Antwerp, Lille, Liefkenshoek, and Hal. Hal was the depot from which the engineer brigades were equipped. The three companies in the Low Countries, before the campaign opened, were the Fourth and Fifth of the Second Battalion, and the Fourth of the Third Battalion. The total strength of the whole ten companies reached the following numbers:—

Sub. Lieuts.	Sergeants.	Corporals.	Second Corp[s].	Drum[s].	Privates.	Total.
10	35	32	42	19	644	782

The Sub-Lieutenants were A. Ross, J. Sparks, W. Stratton, P. Johnston, W. Knapp (died at Tournay, 16th June, 1815), J. Armstrong, A. Turner, C. Gratton, J. Adam, and E. Sanders.

At the Battle of Waterloo, the Royal Sappers and Miners were not engaged. Three companies, however, were brought conveniently near to act in the event of their services being needed; and two companies with the pontoons, were quartered at Malines. Of the former companies, the First company, Fourth Battalion, is considered to have behaved with discredit in quitting the field without sufficient reason, and losing, in the precipitancy and confusion of the march, its baggage and field equipment. But the stigma seems to have been attached to the company without an adequate investigation of the circumstances under which the retreat was imperatively resorted to.

The details of the affair are as follows: On the 17th June the company moved from Hal towards Waterloo, marching the whole of the night, and was in position when the action commenced on the morning of the 18th. After being under fire for some time, it was ordered to the rear by Major Sir George Hoste, and accordingly it marched to the furthest end of the village of Waterloo under Lieutenant W. Faris and Sub-Lieutenant R. Turner. There the company remained till between three and four o'clock p.m., when Lieutenant C. K. Sanders, R.E., joined it.

About this time a brigade of Hanoverian artillery and cavalry, and several of the British cavalry, were retiring. The latter had vainly laboured to penetrate the retreating crowds, and informed Lieutenant Sanders that the French were at the other end of the village. In a wood on the right, discharges of musketry were heard, and both officers and men, who hurried away from the battle, corroborated the general testimony, that the enemy not only had possession of the wood, but in a short time would cut off the British from the road. Still incredulous of the alarming rumours which reached him. Lieutenant Sanders sought more decisive information as to the reported advantages of the French, and at length, satisfied with the additional affirmations of hundreds of officers and soldiers, who threatened in their flight to overrun the company, he at once ordered it to retire.

The circumstances fairly justified this step. But the company had not proceeded far before it was unavoidably thrown into difficulties and disorder. To relieve itself from the masses was impossible. Driven in rear, and encompassed by overwhelming numbers of different regiments, it was borne along at a very rapid rate, in the vortex of the confusion. By the presence of cavalry and cannon, and of capsized waggons and baggage, its march was interrupted and its files broken. Many of the men, therefore, who could not keep up were dispersed among the fugitives; the brigade of waggons, stopped by insuperable obstructions on the road, was abandoned, and the company thus routed lost many of its knapsacks and most of its intrenching tools, baggage, and horses.

Such are the facts of this ill-understood affair, which deserve to be viewed more with regret than animadversion; but Colonel Carmichael Smyth, jealous of the honour of the corps, and feeling this apparent taint upon its character, was highly displeased, and refused to recommend the officers and men of the company for the Waterloo honours and advantages.

★★★★★★★★★★

The only soldier of the corps actually in the battle was Lance-Corporal Henry Donnelly, who was orderly to Major, now Colonel, Oldfield, K.H. He was present on the 17th and 18th, and Colonel Carmichael Smyth, who was seriously indisposed on the night of the 17th, was much indebted to him for his care and attention. His claim to a medal was warmly advocated by the Major, but Colonel Smyth never would allow that he was entitled to it. At the rejection of his just right corporal Donnelly was so much affected, that shortly afterwards he went into hospital and died.

★★★★★★★★★★

Another company ordered to Waterloo on the 18th June, gained much praise for its firmness and regularity in pushing up to the field. This was the eighth company, second battalion, under Sub-Lieutenant Patrick Johnston. At 2 a.m. on the morning of the 18th it marched from Antwerp, and on arrival at Brussels Lieutenant Johnston, finding that the captain of the company as well as the commanding royal engineer and his staff were in the field, at once moved on for Waterloo. Crowds of wounded soldiers, anxious runaways, dismantled waggons and cannon, greatly impeded the march.

From all he met he received the most discouraging advice, but amid the general panic and the numerous obstacles he had to contend with, he resolutely pursued his march and reached the village of Waterloo at 4 o'clock p.m., in a state that reflected great credit upon the discipline and perseverance of the company.

Late in the evening, after firing had ceased, as there were many inducements to plundering and straggling, Lieutenant Johnston withdrew the company a short distance on the Brussels road, and placed it in an empty barn till next morning, when it commenced its march for Paris. In applauding the company for its steadiness and order under trying circumstances, Colonel C. Smyth alluded in a particular manner to the meritorious conduct of Lieutenant Johnston. Neither the officer nor his men were considered entitled to the Waterloo medal and extra service; and for several years afterwards many of the company claimed these advantages with unprecedented pertinacity, but without effect.

The experience of former defects in the Peninsula led to the more perfect organization of the field establishment of the Royal Engineer department. On the 20th June orders to effect the arrangement were issued by Colonel C. Smyth. Every division of the army had one engineer's brigade attached to it; and each brigade consisted of a complete company of well-trained sappers and miners, with drivers, horses and waggons carrying entrenching tools sufficient to employ a working party of 500 men, besides a proportion of artificers' tools, and other engineer stores. The number of companies so distributed was six. A captain and a few subalterns were attached to each brigade, and were responsible for the discipline of the men and efficiency of the horses, &c.

Four companies were attached to the pontoon train, which consisted of eighty pontoons, besides store-waggons, &c, and was drawn by nearly 800 horses, the whole being under the command of Major Tylden, R.E., assisted by a due proportion of captains and subalterns of the same corps. (Pasley's *Elementary Fortification*, 1.) The Second company, Fourth Battalion, under Sub-Lieutenant P. McLean, of sixty-seven total, having joined the army from England soon after the disposition, was also added to the pontoon train.

The total of the engineer establishment with the army and in the Netherlands, under the command of about sixty officers of engineers, amounted to 10 sub-lieutenants and 838 soldiers of the Royal Sappers and Miners, and 550 drivers in charge of 160 waggons, pontoon carriages included, and more than 1,000 horses. Besides medical officers and other non-combatants, and a large force of peasants employed on the works, a small number of Flemish seamen, accustomed to rivers

165

and coasting navigation, was attached to each division of the pontoon train.

The hired drivers, paid at 1s. 6d. a day each and rations, were provided with a uniform of grey clothing, having red cuff and collars to their round jackets; and the Flemish seamen, receiving each an allowance of 2s. a day and rations, were dressed like British sailors, having on the front of their low glazed caps, painted in white, the word "Pontoneer."

All the companies of the corps moved with the army towards Paris, leaving a few small detachments dispersed in Flanders. The second company, second battalion, attached to the first division, was present at the capture of Peronne on the 26th June under Sub-Lieutenant W. Stratton and two captains of engineers. The ladders used on the occasion were collected in the neighbourhood, but being too short were lashed together. The company had the honour of leading the brigade of guards to the assault, (*Elementary Fortification*, 1), and behaved remarkably well. (Gurwood.) Preceding the column, they threw a number of fascines and fagots, hastily prepared by them, into the ditch of the horn-work, and thus enabled the troops to pass its swampy bottom into the body of the place. (Colonel Carmichael Smyth's *Plans of Attack upon Antwerp* &c.)

A party of the company advanced under a heavy fire to force the main entrance. No ladders were carried with it, nor any sledge-hammers or instruments by which to force it open. Daring men were in the batch, and their first impulse, forlorn as they were, urged them to mount the gate. Lieutenant Stratton and Lance-Corporal Edward Councill soon gained the top, and tearing themselves over the spikes which crowned it, jumped into the place, tore down the fastenings, and pulling the gate open, admitted the troops. In leading the stormers into the work. Captain Thomson, R.E., and Lieutenant Stratton were severely wounded, as also two men of the company. Corporal Councill was dangerously wounded in the breast

For the passage of the army to Paris, a pontoon bridge was thrown over the Seine at Argenteuil early in July. Twenty pontoons were employed in its formation, and also some trestles, which were placed next to the banks of the river. On its completion the Duke of Wellington, who was present during the greater part of the operation, first passed over leading his horse, and then the whole army with its artillery and baggage.

From the acute winding of the Seine, it was again necessary to pass the troops over the river, and a pontoon bridge similar to the one laid at Argenteuil was thrown at Aniers. The Fifth company, Second Battalion, and Seventh company, Third Battalion constructed these bridges. Some Flemish seamen assisted in their formation, confining their exertions chiefly to mooring the pontoons. Skilful as they were as sailors, their want of previous training as pontoneers, rendered them far less serviceable than the Royal Sappers and Miners. (Pasley.) The bridges were maintained for some months on the Seine, facilities being afforded for continuing the navigation without interruption.

For this purpose, an opening was made in the centre of each bridge, and when required to be re-established for the passage of the troops, the floating rafts were lashed in their places and removed again when the occasion was served. A sufficient detachment was posted for a season at Chaton, to attend to a similar duty at the bridge thrown there by the Russians. Three companies with forty pontoons were also stationed at Epinay.

After the capture of Paris, the Earl of Mulgrave, then Master-General of the Ordnance, in a letter dated 11th July, expressed his high appreciation of the zealous, able, and beneficial exertions of the officers and soldiers of the corps during the successful progress of the campaign; and also, of the services of the officers and men at the different fortresses.

During the year a number of hired drivers deserted. They were generally ignorant of their duties and many of them of bad character. To take care of the horses was the principal object of the chief engineer and his officers. Obtaining an equal number of foreign drivers to replace the vacancies occasioned by desertion, afforded no promise of advantage or improvement It was therefore, determined, to make an experiment by appointing the Royal Sappers and Miners to the duty.

Accordingly, the number of men required was attached to the horses, and from their peculiar habits of zeal and exertion, they made no difficulty of reconciling themselves to the novel occupation of grooms and drivers. The experiment was eminently successful. The horses were kept efficient and in proper condition; and but for this measure, a number of valuable horses must have been ruined, and the pontoon train, as well as the engineers' brigades, by degrees, have become totally unserviceable. (Pasley.)

At Paris the sappers were called upon to perform a domiciliary visit to the capital, which probably is the only instance on record of British soldiers being so employed in an enemy's country. The Duke

REVIEW OF THE BRITISH TROOPS AT MONTMATRE, NEAR PARIS, BY THE DUKE OF WELLINGTON 21ST OCTOBER 1815

of Wellington having been informed that arms were carried nightly into Paris from Montmartre, desired Sir Thomas Brisbane, commanding the seventh division of the army, to order Captain Harry Jones, R.E. to take the company of sappers attached to the division, with such tools as might be necessary, to examine rigidly every part of Montmartre where it was probable arms might be concealed.

The officer commanding the troops stationed within the intrenchments, had orders not to allow any person to pass out, until Captain Jones had completed his examination. The sappers were employed nearly the whole day in making the search. Every cellar, house, and garden were examined; no place where it was possible to conceal arms was unexplored, but the result was unsuccessful. No doubt, however, existed, that the information communicated to the Duke of Wellington was well founded.

After the capitulation of Paris, the Royal Sappers and Miners were encamped in the vicinity of the city. Late in the year they were removed to other stations on the northern frontiers of France; and until the formation of the army of occupation, were constantly changing their quarters and furnishing detachments for particular services at different places.

To meet the arrangements for reducing the army in France, six companies quitted the country for England in January. Four embarked at Boulogne and two at Calais, the former arrived at Woolwich on the 9th February and the latter on the following day.

Five companies remained with the army of occupation and were attached to divisions as follows:—

1st division	. 8th com., 2nd batt.	. Sub-Lieut. P. Johnson.
2nd division	. 1st com., 3rd batt.	. Sub-Lieut. W. Stevens.
3rd division	. 4th com., 2nd batt.	. Sub-Lieut. J. Adam.
Pontoon train	2nd com., 4th batt.	. Sub-Lieut. W. M'Lean.
	5th com., 2nd batt.	. Sub-Lieut. C. Gratton.

Their united strength counted 435 of all ranks, and they were quartered at Valenciennes, Raismes, Cantain, Bellain, St. Amand, Pernes, Denain, and Houdain. These places were the chief stations of the corps until its removal from France in 1818. Parties were also detached to Cambrai, Hasnon, Racquingham, Blandecque, and St. Pol. Raismes was the headquarters of the pontoon train. Each company attached to the train had twenty pontoons with stores and waggons in charge. The Second company, Fourth Battalion was attached to the right bridge of the train, and the Fifth company, Second Battalion, to the left. The former bridge was permanently stationed at Raismes, but the latter was repeatedly moved from village to village for service and instruction, making its chief halts at Raismes and Aubrey.